THE UNITED STATES OF INCARCERATION

The Criminal Justice Assault on Minorities, the Poor, and the Mentally Ill

Tim Anderson

THE UNITED STATES OF INCARCERATION
THE CRIMINAL JUSTICE ASSAULT ON MINORITIES, THE POOR, AND THE MENTALLY ILL

iUniverse books may be ordered through booksellers or by contacting:

iUniverse
1663 Liberty Drive
Bloomington, IN 47403
www.iuniverse.com
1-800-Authors (1-800-288-4677)

ISBN: 978-1-4917-4626-4 (sc)
ISBN: 978-1-4917-4627-1 (e)

Library of Congress Control Number: 2014916694

Printed in the United States of America.

iUniverse rev. date: 12/15/2014

To Serve and Protect?

Early Warning signs of Fascism

1. Powerful and Continuing Nationalism
2. Disdain for the Recognition of Human Rights
3. Identification of Enemies/Scapegoats as a Unifying Cause
4. Supremacy of the Military
5. Rampant Sexism
6. Controlled Mass Media
7. Obsession with National Security-Homeland
8. Religion and Government are Intertwined
9. Corporate Power is Protected
10. Labor Power is Suppressed
11. Disdain for Intellectuals and the Arts
12. Obsession with Crime and Punishment

A tripling of the prison population in fifteen years is unprecedented in a Democratic society.

—Loic Wacquant

The scales of justice are not balanced in America. In America justice comes into town on the horse you provide.

When buying and selling are controlled by legislation, the first things to be bought and sold are legislators.

—P. J. O'Rourke

Under a government which imprisons any unjustly, the true place for a just man is also a prison.

—Henry David Thoreau

What kind of society spends more on cages than classrooms?

—Rep. Pete Lee (Colorado)

He who opens a school door closes a prison.

—Victor Hugo (1802–1885)

The Author. A former US Marine who also served in the Kentucky, Illinois, and Tennessee National Guard earned his associate's degree in law enforcement technology from Somerset Community College, Bachelor of Science in Physical Education from Eastern Kentucky University and his Master of Science from Eastern Kentucky University. Born November 14, 1966, Tim Anderson grew up in the Near West Side, Chicago, neighborhood of Austin in the '70s and early '80s, and a neighborhood ripe with racial tension. The rise in racial tension led him and his family to move to McCreary County in southeastern Kentucky in the early 1980s. Tim and his siblings had a bird's-eye view of poverty not only in the inner city but in Appalachia as well. He also had a chance to see the biases in criminal justice with regard to being poor and minority status.

Acknowledgments

This book is dedicated to my mother, who died on October 3, 2012, after a short battle with cancer and my Dad Kenneth. To my brothers and sisters, Wendell, Judy, Michael, Donna, Sherry, Grandpa Starling; my son Jared; Milton Ware; Apostolic Faith Church Thirty-Eighth Street, Chicago, Illinois; City of Refuge Christian Fellowship McCreary County, Ky., Victorious Life in Conyers, Ga. Nehemiah Church, Conyers, Ga. McCreary Public Library (Tracy); and Don and Sharon Whitehead. (Sharon, I am blessed to have you tell me years ago, "You're never too old to get an education." Because of this I owe a large part of mine to you.) Special thanks to Terry Gilmore for all the sketches and images in my book, Dr. Pete Kraska and Dr. Kevin Minor and all the criminal justice/ juvenile justice staff at Eastern Kentucky University and to my friend Nada.

The Teachers of the law and the Pharisees brought in a woman caught in adultery. They made her stand before the group

and said to Jesus, "Teacher, this woman
was caught in the act of adultery. In the
Law Moses commanded us to stone
such women. Now what do you say?"
They were using this question as a trap,
in order to have a basis for accusing him.

But Jesus bent down and started to write on the
ground with his finger. When they kept on questioning
him, he straightened up and said to them, "Let any one
of you who is without sin be the first to throw a stone at
her." Again he stooped down and wrote on the ground.
At this, those who heard began to go away one at a
time, the older ones first, until only Jesus was left, with
the woman still standing there. Jesus straightened up
and asked her, "Woman, where are they? Has no one
condemned you?" "No one, sir," she said. "Then neither
do I condemn you," Jesus declared. "Go now and leave
your life of sin." **John 8:1-11**

Sadly, our society, which was built on Christian
values, has gone astray from the teachings of Jesus.
We reside in a society that has forgotten grace and
mercy. In fact, over the last forty years we have become
excessively harsh, not to killers and armed robbers but
to nonviolent drug offenders and the mentally ill who
were once treated in rehab and psychiatric facilities
but are now being warehoused in iron cages due to
defunding.

Key Terms

Fordist-Keyneysian Era- From the late-1940s onwards, the economies of the industrialized nations enjoyed continuous growth, with pay and profits steadily growing in parallel. However, in the early-1970s, the rate of growth suddenly went into decline. In part, this decline in the economy was caused by the revolt against the disciplines of the assembly-lines. Simultaneously, a rapid rise in the price of oil and other raw materials greatly increased the costs of production for most businesses. As in prior decades, national governments reacted to the crisis by adopting reflationary policies. But, unlike in earlier recessions, this Fordist strategy didn't work. Instead, the global economy went into a period of persistent inflation, currency instability and growing unemployment. This failure in economic policy was a result of the globalization of production. For over three decades, U.S., European and Japanese companies had been slowly expanding to obtain economies of scale on an international level. Outside the control of any one national government, the global trading system created by these multinationals was regulated by the world financial markets. Following the fall of fixed exchange rates, the international competition between different monetary systems increasingly decided the internal economic policies of the industrialized nations. For example, reflation in a single country was prevented by balance of payments crises, which forced a return to deflationary policies. Once the governments of the industrialized countries lost control over their own national economies, the virtuous circle of rising production and consumption was broken. Instead of steadily increasing wages and welfare benefits, workers now faced cuts in social benefits, stagnant money wages and mass unemployment. Faced with the reemergence of the social problems of the past, new ideas had to be found to tackle the growing crisis of Fordism.

Neo-conservatism

A large amount of confusion exists concerning neo-conservatism and neo-liberalism. They both refer to ideologies of international affairs and are not related to the commonly known social philosophies of "conservatism" and "liberalism." For example, a vast number of social conservatives believe completely in philosophies of neo-liberalism, and most politicians adhere to a combination of both neo-conservatism and neo-liberalism. (Neo-conservatism) Irving Kristol was an American, journalist, columnist and author who is thought by some to be the founding father of neo-conservatism (Right Web 2009). Neo-conservatism is a component of American conservatism that includes support of political individualism, free markets, the assertive fostering of democracy, and U.S. national interest in international affairs via military means. Neo-conservative doctrine believes in utilizing the state to work actively to attain conservative goals. While most neoconservatives still support small government, they contend that the government must work assertively in some areas, such as criminal justice, to foster conservative beliefs and policies. However, while they downsize other areas of government they usually expand the correctional and military components (Konsczal 2012; Ehrman 2011; Western 2004).

From a correctional standpoint, neoconservatives say that they are the party of law and order. The contemporary law and order movement launched in 1964 with Barry Goldwater's speech accepting the Republican bid for the presidency. Then a small issue, law and order had a particular ring in the South, where George Wallace's following was growing with a similar platform. While Goldwater suffered a huge loss in the election, he did very well among Southern states using this platform, something Richard Nixon would strategically utilize in the following presidential election. The emergence of modern conservative politics defunded the welfare system and put in place an expressive politics of criminal justice. It was in this vein that rehabilitation replaced retribution. Three-strikes-and-you're-out laws, minimum mandatory sentences, the War on Drugs, and the mass imprisonment of minorities and the poor are watermarks of the neoconservative movement (Western 2004; Konsczal 2012; Karmen 1990).

Neo-liberalism

Neo-liberalism (corporate capitalism, corporate globalism, and even referred to as suicide economics) is poisonous talk of criminalization and punishment that legitimizes states that have faltered on their promise to the social wage. The neoliberal government has a stake in phobia of crime and convincing the public of imminent danger by exaggerating and inflating or distorting crime statistics. But the overarching tactic is to sell citizens on the idea that law enforcement and punishment are the solutions to all social-economic problems. In America, the fear-of-crime debate terrorizes every election, and media anxiety because of crime competes with coverage with the weather. This strategy has been extremely potent because citizens are now in the control of neoliberal criminal justice philosophy. A philosophy that believes there is seemingly no issue that can't be remedied with more law enforcement, more correctional facilities, and increased punishment (George 2013; O'Malley 2008; Monahan 2006; Philomena 2001; Loo 2013).

The word neo-liberalism was first coined in the 1930s by the Freiburg School of German economists. It referenced the doctrine that was extremely moderate in contrast to traditional liberalism, both in its disdain for laissez-faire politics that stressed humanistic values. Michel Foucault defined neo-liberalism as, a method of ruling that does not ask the government what liberty it will leave to the economy but asks the economy how its freedom can have a government-creating function and role—in the sense that the economy will make possible the foundation of the state's legitimacy. When government intervenes in the functioning of markets, it isn't to rectify injustices but instead it is to create further and maintain and expand the vitality of the economy itself. When neo-liberalism calls for the government to leave markets to their natural order, it redirects the function of the states power. The redirection is on the regulation of activities that lie outside the formal market (Foucault 1978, 1979; Taylor and Jordan 2009; Konsczal 2012).

Wacquant's Neoliberal State

The fall of the Fordist-Keynesian model starting in the middle part of the 1970s gave birth to the rise of neo-liberalism. Loic Wacquant a French sociologist, specializing in urban sociology, urban poverty, racial inequality, the body, social theory and ethnography describes the neoliberal state in four components: economic deregulation, a welfare state descent, disavowing, and reorganization. It is the rise of a growing, intrusive, and proactive criminal justice system and implementation of the societal expression of individual responsibility. It is dogmatic in the ideology that how one succeeds or fails in life is up to the individual. Opposite of the neoliberal talk, we see a double-headed/schizophrenic creature; that is liberal and excessively permissive for the rich and middle classes however, very strict and harsh in its punishment for the economically disadvantaged and underprivileged. For example, The North American Free Trade Agreement essentially deregulated Corporate America and took jobs from Americans. Then told those people to get a job or go to prison (Wacquant 2010; Campbell 2010; Mead 2004).

The punitive transformation of prison policy in America post–civil rights reacts not to increasing criminal insecurity. Rather to social insecurity brought on by the collapse of wage labor and the shake-up of the ethnic- racial chain of command. It is a wider remolding of the government bonding restrictive workfare and growing prison fare under the ideology of moral behaviorism. This paternalistic service of the criminalization of poverty desires to slow the urban chaos brought on by economic deregulation and to force precarious labor on the postindustrial worker. It also props up a disturbing theater of civic morality on whose political elites can mastermind the public condemnation of deviant people. For example the teenage welfare mom, the hooded street thug, the wandering sex predator, and close the legitimacy deficit they endure when they abandon the historical government goal of socioeconomic protection. Punishing the poor is not simply a technical implement for police but a central political institution, and it shows that the capitalist revolution from above called neo-liberalism is made up of not just the advent of limited government but the erecting of an overgrown and intrusive prison nation deeply hurtful to the principles of democracy (Wacquant 2009).

"**Prison–Industrial Complex**" (**PIC**) is used to attribute the rapid expansion of the US inmate population to the political influence of private prisons and businesses that supply goods and services to government prison agencies Such groups include corporations that contract prison labor, construction companies, surveillance technology vendors, companies that operate prison food services and medical facilities, private probation companies, attorneys, and lobbyist that represent them. Activist groups contend that the prison-industrial complex is perpetuating a misguided belief that incarceration is an effective answer to social problems i.e., mental illness, illiteracy homelessness, unemployment, and drug abuse. The promotion of prison-building as a job creator and the use of inmate labor are also cited as elements of the prison-industrial complex. The term often implies a network of actors who are motivated by making profit rather than solely by punishing or rehabilitating criminals or reducing crime rates. Supporters of this view believe that the desire for financial gain has led to the expansion of the corrections industry and incarceration rates (Davis, 1998 Friedman, 2012).

INTRODUCTION

Every weapon made, every warship launched, every rocket fired signifies, in the final sense a theft from those who are without food, those who are cold and without clothes. This planet in arms is not just spending money. It is wasting the sweat of its laborers, the genius of its scientists, and the hopes of its youth. This is no way of life at all. Under the gloom of threatening conflict, it is humanity hanging from a cross of iron (Eishenhower 1961). In Dwight Eisenhower's presidential farewell address in 1961, he cautioned that the Cold War was enabling weapons makers, military strategists, scientific experts, and legislative insiders to mold a poisonous and toxic alliance of convenience. Steered by mutually enriching self-interests under patriotic talk of fighting Communism, Eisenhower was concerned that this modern formation of political power could become so large that it could collapse democracy. The same can be said of the prison industrial complex. Every prison erected, every assault rifle utilized by prison guards, every flak jacket and helmet made for swat teams and correctional facilities is a theft from the hungry. It is a theft from the unclothed, from money that could be used for education and health care. In the mid-1980's as the cold war was coming to an end, Ronald Reagan gave his famous "tear this wall down speech' at the Berlin Wall. He did as America was simultaneously erecting our own walls of bondage known as the *Prison Industrial Complex*.

Many experts in the criminal justice field are giving a dire warning of America's prison system. The simple fact is, crime is big business, a growth industry so to speak, and a large part of the American economy has become woven in with the obsession to incarcerate. Judges, prosecutors, parole, probation officers, drug task forces, prisons, universities and professors who teach criminal justice rely in no small part on criminals and the threat of crime for their vitality. Over the last several years US citizens, some of them just kids, have been detained and charged with looking for Indian artifacts on government land. Some teens have been adjudicated into the system for tossing peanuts on school transportation and sitting on a milk crate. One citizen was indicted for lying about their address to get their children in a better school district. One woman had her home taken by a drug task force. She was renting part of her house to a family member to help him get on his feet. Completely unaware he was dealing drugs. Because of asset forfeiture tied to drug laws she lost everything she has worked for. In the meantime, HSBC laundered money for Mexican drug lords; Goldman Sachs created and sold mortgage deals that were intended to flop. Bank of America and Lehman Brothers stashed billions of dollars in bonuses and loans from investors and received little or no punishment. Attorney General Eric Holder decided it would be detrimental to prosecute HSBC because it could damage the economy (Bucheit 2013; Palaez, 2013).

The myth of the American justice system in is that everyone is treated fairly, regardless of their color or economic status. The ideology that no one is above the law is a good one in theory. However, like many great ideas, the truth, usually, lags far behind the talk. It is very apparent by examining the criminal justice terrain that minorities and the poor are unfairly targeted in the criminal justice system. This is nothing new, however. Inequality has been in existence in the criminal justice apparatus since the birth of the nation. However, our society has come up with new and innovative methods in which to do it (Wright 2013; Davis 2008).

Some of these methods began to take root in the latter part of the 1960s as the U.S. correctional system embarked on a journey of institutional transformation.

Changes in the structure of society and politics prompted transformations in criminal justice, with enormous results for the quality of freedom. The American criminal justice system turned its back on rehabilitation, and by the 1970s, policy makers were doubtful that prisons could hinder crime by reforming offenders. Incarceration was not used so much for rehabilitation but rather for detaining, deterrence, and punishment. The public, influenced by the media and politicians, believed that America's criminal justice system was too lenient, and correctional reforms were needed. As a result, America is now the harshest and most punitive industrialized nation in the world. We incarcerate five times more people per capita than England, nine times more than Germany, and twelve times more than Japan (Equal Justice Initiative 2010; Western 2005). This obsession to use prisons to deal with social problems began when America started to expand the powers of police agencies around the nation, generating by the 1970s an unheralded dependence on imprisonment to treat it's sociopolitical, financial, and mental health problems. This was done so by labeling new acts as crimes and by enhancing the harshness of sentencing for other acts (Corrections Project 2013; Kraska and Brent 2011; McCann 2007).

Incarcerated Americans (1920-2010)

Year		Prison Pop.
2010		*2,500,000*
2000	**(2003 Half the States Enacted Three strikes laws)**	*1,500,000*
1990	**(1996 Welfare to Work)**	*1,000,000*
1980	**(1984 Sentencing Reform Act)**	*500,000*
1970	**(1971 War On Drugs)**	*400,000*
1950		*47,000*
1930		*47,000*
<u>1920</u>		*<u>13,000</u>*

A large section of the general public now believes that most people who are sent to prison are killers, sexual predators, and armed robbers. However, over 50 percent of the offenders incarcerated are in prison for drug crimes, and a big portion of those incarcerated are for nonviolent crimes. In the past three decades, there has been a 500 percent increase in the amount of US citizens behind bars. For years, our country has nurtured a massive prison infrastructure that mirrors and solidified a distinctly harsh and merciless idea of justice, one embedded in our national consciousness. We recently resided in a nation where, in a nationally televised debate, the audience applauded a front-running presidential hopeful for having governed over a record amount of executions. We reside in a nation where it is readily accepted under the banner of order and safety that hundreds of thousands of minorities must endure the humiliation of being illegally stopped, questioned and searched by law enforcement. The asinine prosecution of a mother for the sad, accidental death of her child due to jaywalking and another for enrolling her child in the wrong district in a desperate desire for a quality education becomes little more than fodder for the news media. A life sentence for stealing a bottle of vitamins or for a nonviolent marijuana offense, because of previous convictions, hardly raises an eyebrow. They are a component of a system that fuels off of punishing people severely, pandering to a mind-set that ignores collective responsibility for the least among us. Telling large numbers of people in communities all over the nation they don't matter (Noisette 2012; Anisette 2012; Marable 2008; LAO 2005). Tragically, much of the modern criminal justice policy has been fueled by legislation legitimized by questionable data concerning the crime problem in America. The news media, Hollywood "law and order pornography," neo-liberalism and neo-conservatism have been some of the major contributors to the correctional explosion (Pratt 2009; May, Minor Ruddel, and Matthews 2008).

How the Criminal Justice System Creates Social Misfits

Over the last thirty years, the institutional demographics of U.S. social inequality have evolved because of the fast growth in the correctional population. U.S. prisons and jails have generated a modern social group, a group of societal misfits who are joined by the common experience of imprisonment, crime, economic disadvantage, racial minority status, and nominal education. As a rogue group, the men and women in our correctional facilities have decreased access to the social advancement available to the mainstream. Social and financial disadvantage, crystallizing in correctional confinement, is maintained over the life course and carried on from one generation to another. There is a deep institutionalized inequality that has renewed race and class disadvantage (Western and Pettit 2010).

The influence of the correctional system on social and financial disadvantage is apparent in the economic and family lives of ex-felons. The social inequality generated by mass imprisonment is large and lasting for three central reasons: (1) it is hidden, (2) it is cumulative, and (3) it is intergenerational. The inequality is hidden in the sense that institutionalized populations frequently lie outside or official accounts of financial well-being. Inmates, though taken from the lowest parts of society, appear in no measures of economic disadvantage or unemployment. As a result, the full degree of the disadvantage of those with high imprisonment rates is underestimated. The inequality is cumulative due to the social and economics that flow from imprisonment is accrued by people who already have minimal economic opportunities. Mass imprisonment thus worsens disadvantage and stops mobility for the most disadvantaged in society. Lastly, criminal justice inequalities are intergenerational, impacting not only those who are sent to correctional facilities but their families and offspring as well, sometimes for many generations (Western and Pettit 2010; Wright 2013).

A Dire Warning of the Prison-Industrial Complex

At the start of the century, America experienced an unparalleled economic explosion, with low rates of unemployment, an increasing standard of living, the federal surplus, and a robust state budget. Crime statistics decreased steadily in each country every year from 1992 through the present. However, in spite of these positive cycles, there is every indication that the evolution toward punitive justice and security enhancement is continuing at full strength. As the market in privatized security grows, the delivery of correctional policy gains speed and the crime industrial machine replicates itself. We are staring down the barrel of the potential of being detained in a modern iron cage. The modern culture of crime suppression, originating from phobias and anxieties of the latter part of the twentieth century, may very well extend way after its original conditions have stopped. Such arrangements spur institutional investments and generate guaranteed benefits, especially for the elite groups that are the furthest distance from them. They offer a method of allocating the price of crime, unfair and unbalanced, but capable nonetheless. Correctional solutions may come at a high cost. However, the last two and a half decades have proven that the price tag can be carried even when citizens are notoriously apprehensive to meet the price of other public funding (Kraska and Brent 2011).

The research sector of the American Congress is warning of the 30 years of historically unparalleled growth in the amount of people imprisoned in the United States. They are saying that it has led to a level of overcrowding that is now damaging the infrastructure of the American federal prisons. According to new research by the Congressional Research Service (CRS), federal prison populations have leaped from 25,000 to 219,000 prisoners, a growth of almost 790 percent. Swollen by such figures, for decades America has imprisoned far more people than any other nation, currently incarcerating about 716 people out of every 100,000 citizens. In 1980, the federal correctional system housed 24,000 people at a price of $333 million. Since that time, the federal prison population skyrocketed with a 700 percent growth to 217,000 inmates. A yearly price tag of $6 billion, a 1,700 percent increase in spending (ABA 2013; Biron 2013).

Incarceration has become the first reaction for entirely too many of the social issues that plague people who are in the grip of poverty. These societal ills are frequently disguised by being conveniently placed together under the category "crime" and by the automatic attribution of criminality to minorities. Homelessness, unemployment, substance abuse, psychological disorders, and illiteracy are, but a number of the issues that vanish from society's view when the people are contending with them are reduced to cages. Correctional facilities give the appearance of performing a magic trick. However, correctional facilities do not make problems disappear—they make human beings disappear. And the act of removing large amounts of individuals from indigent, immigrant, and racially marginalized neighborhoods has also become big business. However, the apparent ease of magic always hides a large amount of behind-the-scenes work. When correctional facilities make humans vanish in order to portray the misguided belief of fixing social problems, correctional infrastructures must be designed to accommodate a rapidly expanding population of imprisoned people. Programs, goods, and services have to be offered to keep jailed populations alive. Often these populations have to be kept busy, and in other instances (especially in oppressive super-maximum facilities and in INS facilities), keeping them from almost all meaningful activity. Large amounts of handcuffed and shackled individuals are transferred across state lines taken from one state or federal prison to another. All this activity, which was in the past the main duty of the state, is presently outsourced by private organizations. Their connections to government in the field of what is euphemistically labeled "corrections" reverberate alarmingly with the military-industrial complex. The payoffs that accumulate from investment in the correctional industry, like those that accrue from investment in arms production, only end in social destruction. Considering the foundational similarities and profitability of business-government linkages in the areas of military production and public punishment, the growing correctional system can be labeled the "Prison-Industrial Complex" (Davis 1998).

What Is the Prison-Industrial Complex?

Since the prison-industrial complex is such a large and wide system, it's often helpful to dissect it into sections. What follows is an analysis of the core components of the prison-industrial complex, although its arms stretch way beyond these basic features. "Prison-industrial complex" is a phrase we use to define the overlapping interests of government and industry that utilize surveillance, policing, and incarceration. As solutions to what are, in all reality, socioeconomic and political issues (Critical Resistance 2014).

Criminalization

Criminalization is the procedure through which certain activities become criminal. Actions become illegal only after they have been culturally or legally described as such through processes via laws, court rulings, or institutional policies. Ideas about what is criminal extend way past specific actions, however. Criminalization is also what happens when whole categories of citizens, or of particular social circumstances (the homeless, youth, immigrants), are targeted by police agencies for surveillance, punishment, and control. The criminalization of homelessness, for instance, includes the control of homeless people through legislation that make everything from public urination, sleeping in the park to participation in informal economies (i.e., street vending in big metropolitan areas like New York) illegal and punishable (Herzing; Critical Resistance 2014).

The criminalization of women who are addicted drugs includes potent new legislation that can send pregnant females to jail if a physician or hospital reports proof of drug use while pregnant. In some states, legislation that impose a permanent ban on access to financial assistance and government housing for individuals convicted of drug-related crimes also criminalize economically disadvantaged women. Rather than viewing addiction as a public health issue, physicians are turned into informants, and patients into criminals. The criminalization of adolescents of color includes the direct incorporation of law enforcement into school security. It also incorporates legislation in numerous cities that ban young people from gathering in groups (as little as three people) on the street and news images that portray young minorities as out-of-control super predators. Under the current criminal justice system, fundamental social activities become overlaid with a cloud of suspicion (Herzing; Critical Resistance 2014).

The criminalization of illegal aliens and immigrants contributes to racial profiling, unjustified stop and frisk of noncitizens and immigrants, as well as deportation, detention, and incarceration. The process of criminalization is a vital part of the prison-industrial complex. It is but one of the components that make it possible for police agencies and the courts to aim its efforts at not just specific actions but specific categories of people. While preserving a public body that believes that criminals are a danger to them and their families (Herzing; Critical Resistance 2014).

Criminalization also contributes to the illusion that social, political, and economic problems are law enforcement problems. That safety of all sorts, including economic security, can be preserved by watching, controlling, and detaining certain categories of individuals who suffer most under structural inequalities, such as being poor or racism. By basing an idea of what and who is "criminal" and strengthening that notion through use of news agencies and governmental legislation. The prison-industrial complex can have social and physical power over those people identified as criminals. For example, the indigent, minorities, people with psychiatric problems, political opponents, and immigrants (Herzing 2005; Critical Resistance 2014).

Media

The vitality of the prison-industrial complex relies in no small part on the illusions of crime and punishment delivered by the media. The media have been a key component in solidifying who and what we define as criminal, what proper reactions are to criminal acts, as well as creating and enhancing feelings of fear and vulnerability among those watching. A 1996 ABC News poll found that 76 percent of the public stated they develop their concepts about crime as a result of media stories. However, just 22 percent based their ideas on data gained through personal experience (Herzing 2005; Critical Resistance 2014).

In a procedure similar to that of criminalization, who we view in the news as "criminals" and what actions we see as "criminal" are by the priorities of corporate America and politicians. These power players utilize news outlets as a method of disseminating their messages. Films, TV, radio programs, newspaper/ magazine stories and entire publications devoted to issues linked to the prison-industrial complex as well as the consistency of the images utilized portray violence, crime, and punishment to dictate, what people and situations become the focus of our suspicion i.e., minorities and economically disadvantaged people. News consumers are given a diet of images and ideas of what the correct responses to those individuals and circumstances should be—for example, surveillance, aggressive policing, strict sentencing, and incarceration. The main media images of "crime" and "criminals" regularly place African American and (to a slightly smaller extent) Hispanic males at the core of criminal activities, enhancing the targeting of these groups for criminalization and punishment. Furthermore, because the prevailing news images of responses to "criminal" actions are excessive force or harassment and incarceration. They hinder what alternatives we believe are at our disposal (Herzing 2005; Critical Resistance 2014).

Surveillance

Surveillance, or the keen supervision of an individual or group under suspicion, is the main strategy of the prison-industrial complex. Physical and electronic surveillance, including video, audio, mail, and e-mail surveillance is utilized to monitor people's communications and physical activities. Surveillance is utilized in some instances as a fear tactic. Especially in the case of political dissidents, the threat of surveillance is in some cases used to encourage citizens to censor what they say as well as their actions. One of the primary methods of surveillance is the utilization of informants to get access to groups being monitored. They establish relationships with people for the sole purpose of securing data concerning (and frequently disturbing the activities of) those under suspicion (Herzing 2005; Critical Resistance 2014).

Groups of individuals who are exposed to public scrutiny by virtue of their inability to obtain individualized private spaces (i.e., the homeless, street vendors, and youth) are especially vulnerable to surveillance by law enforcement and business owners and are frequently targeted by police agencies. Immigrants have long been the objects of surveillance and suspicion in America at borders and immigration locations, via contact with the INS and through their employers. One example is the growing utilization of community watch programs and neighborhood policing where citizens are encouraged by local law enforcement agencies to spy on their neighbors with suspicion and report any unusual activities to police. Since 9/11 police agencies' utilization of surveillance has increased substantially, particularly under the PATRIOT Act (Herzing 2005; Critical Resistance 2014).

Surveillance is the central piece to the prison-industrial complex in targeting specific people and groups of people and molding the criminalization and punishment methods used against them. Surveillance, especially electronic surveillance, is also pushed as an effective "crime-fighting" tactic. However, no link has been established between utilization of surveillance and decreased crime rates. The utilization of surveillance as a weapon of law enforcement emphasizes the unbalanced distributions of power and wealth upon which the prison-industrial complex is founded. Who gets monitored, who is suspicious, and who gets into the prison-industrial complex as a result of monitoring. These all contribute to the phobia that is so critical to solidifying the centrality of the prison-industrial complex in dealing with the problems generated by these inequities (Herzing; Critical Resistance 2014).

Policing

The decisions law enforcement agencies make about whom to target, what to target them for, when to arrest and book them play a key role in who ultimately goes to jail. As we have seen, those decisions are also made within the greater picture of a system of policing that is designed to target the economically disadvantaged, minorities and immigrants, individuals who do not play along to what is considered socially acceptable behavior in public or in their homes. For instance, law enforcement regularly target females, homosexuals, minorities, and youth simply based on their looks or behavior. On the surface, it may appear that law enforcement is out on the beat to hinder or solve "crime"—their mere presence is a method of enforcing societal control. Policing incorporates violence to preserve its systemic power, as well as the individual power of officers (Herzing 2005; Critical Resistance 2014).

All throughout political histories of resistance in America, the battle against police brutality is frequently at the top of the list. Not only does law enforcement utilize the threat of violence—the firearms on their hips, the billy clubs on their belts—to control people. They also frequently utilize force to make stops, inquiries, and arrests. When individuals are killed at the hands of law enforcement, more often than not, the government summarizes that the utilization of force is reasonable. These attitudes give extraordinary discretion to individual officers and the organizations that train them. Police violence also comes in other ways for instance, harassment of people on the street or stop-and-search practices, stopping people with no cause to frisk them for drugs or weapons. These are methods frequently utilized to control and supervise economically disadvantaged people and minorities. While some supporters contend that law enforcement abuse is a minor issue that can be blamed on the actions of bad police. It is, in fact, a systemic issue that is inherent to the way the policing system in America is established and preserved. The consistency of the issue within varied communities nationwide, as well as the incompetence of review boards and the lack of attention to the problem at every level of policing (from the local to the federal) paint a picture of the systemic nature of the issue (Herzing 2005; Critical Resistance 2014).

To Serve and Protect?

The final days of colonialism taught America's revolutionaries that armies in the streets bring conflict and tyranny. As a result, our nation has, for the most part, labored to keep the military out of law enforcement. However, over the last three decades, America's police have increasingly come looking like ground troops. The results have been dire: the home is no longer a place of safe haven. The Fourth Amendment dismantled and law enforcement today has been trained to see the citizens they serve as an enemy. In recent years, the militarization of law enforcement has grown substantially. Today's armored-up law enforcement is a far cry from the constables of early America. The turbulence of the 1960s brought about the invention of the SWAT team, which in turn led to the start of military tactics in the ranks of law enforcement. President Nixon's War on Drugs, Ronald Reagan's fight against poverty, Bill Clinton's COPS program, the post-9/11 security state under Bush and Obama—by degrees, each of these innovations grew. As they grew they gave more power to police forces, always at the price of freedom. And these are just several among a number of reckless programs. Not only has the character of the police come to resemble more closely that of the American military, but it is also being equipped with the same technologies. SWAT (special weapons and tactics) teams are possibly the most dramatic example of the crossroads of police and military technologies and practices in American policing. From giving training in tactics and instruction in utilizing certain kinds of equipment to the cooperation amongst the military and domestic police at the American/Mexican border. Militarization of the police has meant that America has become another arena where the military can function and has meant that American citizens are possible military targets to be eliminated. The model that the military utilizes for problem solving (eliminating targets) is just not appropriate to the role that law enforcement theoretically offers. The appropriate role is to serve the needs of the neighborhoods in which they operate (Critical Resistance 2014; Balko 2013; Herzing 2005; Kraska and Kappeler 1997).

The slogan of police units in previous generations was to serve and protect. However, in contemporary society law enforcement has increasingly become an oppressive tool of the government. Militarism influences many aspects of social life, particularly in cultures like America that put great emphasis on military might. Much like the medicalization of social problems becomes entangled with social rationale and problem construction outside the medical profession, so does militarization impact many aspects of the molding of and response to social issues outside of the military. Recent developments show the astounding effect the war slogan has on a critical component of governmental activity outside of the military—the criminal justice system. The armed forces model is the building blocks for prison boot camps, the War on Drugs, the war on terror, etc. (Kraska and Kappeler 1997; Balko 2013).

The militarization of the police was never more apparent than in the Boston bombings. Former Rep. Ron Paul (R-Texas) concluded that, the reaction of police officials to the attack should scare citizens more than the attack itself. Paul compared the large-scale search for suspect Dzhokhar Tsarnaev to images from a military coup in a distant banana republic. Citizens witnessed the forced lockdown of Boston, quasi-military police driving tanks in the streets and house to house armed searches without warrants. Families tossed out of their residences at gunpoint searched without cause, businesses forced to shut down, and transportation being brought to a halt. These were not the pictures from a military coup in a far-off banana republic, but rather the scenes in Boston as Americans got a sampling of martial law. The apparent reason for the military-style takeover of sections of Boston was that the accused perpetrator of a terrible crime was at large. The Boston bombing offered the chance for the government to turn what simply should have been a law enforcement investigation into a military-style takeover of an American city (Siddiqui, 2013).

Courts

The judicial system is incredibly overworked, with thousands of people all over the nation who can't afford to post bail waiting for their day in court, detained in some cases for a year or more. Court-appointed lawyers who offer services to individuals who cannot pay for attorneys are frequently dealing with immense workloads. For example, the recommended yearly workload for a court-appointed attorney should not be more than 150 felonies, 400 misdemeanors, 200 juvenile cases. However, in Pittsburgh, Pennsylvania, public defenders are handling between 600 and 1,100 cases annually. When cases finally make it to trial, juries are selected through a strategic process where both sides attempt to eliminate individuals who might lean toward one or the other side. Often district attorneys eliminate those individuals who have had any bad interactions with the police or may be inclined to sympathize with the person or people on trial. Court cases are hardly ever heard by the "peers" of those standing trial. Because the judicial system is just one point in the whole system that puts people behind bars, it mirrors the problems that start in other parts of the system. As minorities and economically disadvantaged people are targeted for surveillance and police oppression, more of those same people wind up on trial. The entire prison-industrial complex is molded by structural inequalities, so it follows that the judicial system targets minorities and poor people just like every other component of the prison-industrial complex (Herzing 2005; Critical Resistance 2014).

Prisons

Correctional facilities are the ultimate expression of the prison-industrial complex. In their very design, correctional facilities are intended to create settings of complete surveillance and absolute physical control. Correctional facilities are also designed to isolate. The trend in prison construction appears to be toward limiting interaction amongst inmates so that people incarcerated have little chance to interact with people other than correctional officers, further contributing to the dehumanizing impact of incarceration. The growing trend toward super-maximum prisons (prisons that control prisoners through harsh social isolation, limited movement, and an environment with limited stimulation and the utilization of solitary confinement and control units within correctional facilities and some jails) should remind us of the real reason behind incarceration—punishment and control (Herzing 2005; Critical Resistance 2014).

The Correctional Metamorphosis
Faulty Research

In the latter part of the nineteenth century, the rehabilitative mantle transformed from redeeming sinners to philosophies based in the Progressive Era's faith in the social sciences. They did so by utilizing targeted and rational therapy to "repair" offenders who had been "broken" by poverty and other societal ills. It was this platform upon which academic criminology and the contemporary criminal justice system were founded—at least for most of the twentieth century. At the beginning of the 1970s, the primacy of rehabilitation came under scrutiny from two distinct angles. Both of which disagreed with the idea that criminals were "malfunctioning" because of negative social conditions (Allen 1981; Garland 2001; Moyers 2007)

On one hand, a section of academics contended that many offenders—particularly members of minority groups—were rightfully fighting against an oppressive society. That rehabilitation was the system's attempt to force bourgeois values on possible revolutionaries. On the other, an increasing group of criminologists noted that rehabilitation services tended to have a nominal impact on recidivism rates. They contended that offenders were rational actors for whom the criminal justice system should be created to deter. One such criminologist, Robert Martinson, wrote a research paper called "Nothing Works," and it became the battle cry of those against rehabilitation or rehabilitative philosophy and had influenced some in steering citizens away from liberal programs of rehabilitation and toward retribution or deterrence as justifications for punishment. In 1974 D. Lipton, Robert Martinson, and J. Wilks, using meta-analysis, analyzed every evaluation of criminal rehabilitation programs between 1945 and 1967. They summarized that with few and isolated exceptions, the rehabilitative attempts reported so far have had no significant impact on reoffending. The results of this analysis persuaded them that not much seems to be effective, and one program wasn't more efficient than another (Allen 1981; Garland 2001; Moyers 2007).

Although support for rehabilitation services remains high for nonviolent offenders, poll results since the 1980s implied that most citizens no longer see rehabilitation itself as the central purpose of the criminal justice system. Indeed, numerous states now have minimum sentencing legislation mandating certain punishments regardless of what the circumstances of the crime are. Scholars have implied that this "decline of the rehabilitative paradigm" can be ascribed to opportunistic people. Politicians utilizing the crime issue as a political hot button to win elections, sensationalized accounts of violent crime in the news, the growing perception that the social order is collapsing, and the identification of crime with racial minorities (Allen 1981; Garland 2001; Moyers 2007).

War on Drugs

The antidrug legislation of the state acted as a spear and screen for a war against individuals viewed as the least useful and possibly most threatening components of the population. For example, paperless immigrants, the unemployed, the homeless, beggars, vagrants and other societal misfits who are seen as useless to society (Wacquant 1999). President Ronald Reagan officially launched the modern drug war in 1982, when drug crime was decreasing, not increasing. From the very beginning, the war had little to do with the drug crime and almost everything to do with racial politics. The drug effort was a component of a large and extremely successful Republican Party tactic of utilizing racially coded political appeals on topics of crime and welfare. It hoped to draw indigent and working-class Caucasian voters who were angry about, and threatened by, desegregation, busing, and affirmative action (Alexander 2010).

Several years after the drug war started, crack cocaine went out on the streets of urban communities. The Reagan administration grabbed hold of this development with joy, employing staffs who were to be responsible for publicizing urban crack babies, crack moms, crack whores, and drug-connected crimes. The mission was to make urban crack abuse and violence a media spectacle. To solidify public support for the drug war, this would prompt Congress to dedicate millions of dollars in extra expenditures to it. For over a decade, African American drug dealers and users were frequently in media stories that would saturate the evening TV news. Congressional and state politicians all over the nation would dedicate billions of dollars to the drug initiative and pass severe mandatory minimum sentences for drug offenses, sentences lengthier than murderers receive in many countries (Alexander 2010).

The March of the Neoliberals

By the middle part of the 1970s, the neoliberal goal, geared to decreasing the welfare state and redistributing income upward, started to have an effect. Traditional liberal political ideology in support of an expanded welfare system had steered American social welfare policy since the 1930s, when the fall of the economy prompted the evolution of the welfare state. However, another big crisis in the mid-1970s gave birth to the neoliberal ideology. Neo-liberalism, the main reaction to the second economic crisis of the twentieth century, came to the forefront in America in the mid-1970s. It did so when Jimmy Carter ran for the Democratic Party's nomination on an anti-Washington battle cry. Several years later in 1981, President Reagan stated the taxing authority of the state must be utilized to generate money for legitimate government reasons and cannot be utilized to regulate the economy or bring about social transformation. Well known as "Reaganomics," neo-liberalism was ignited in full by the Reagan administration and performed to a different extent by every presidential administration since then. Neoliberalism looks to recapture the primacy of the market and dismantle both the New Deal and the Great Society social services. Neoliberalism redefined the playbook governing the relationship between business, people, and the government (Donnough, Reich, and Kotz 2010; Bresler 2008; Abromovitz 2012).

President Bill Clinton (1996) stated that the period of large government was finished. The tactic was rooted in tax and spending being slashed. In the 1980s, neoliberal agendas could be seen in reforms of law enforcement, sentencing, and correctional practice. Law enforcement had to begin innovative managerial principles. These were associated with outsourcing numerous duties, such as transporting inmates and operating red-light cameras, performing security work under contract, etc. Greater emphasis placed on the personal responsibility of offenders. The centrality of welfare rehabilitation issues in sentencing and corrections started to transform in favor of a more retributive stance. Many questioned if it had ever been effective in reforming criminals, fostering a greater emphasis on more cost-efficient blueprints of imprisonment (Abromovitz 2012; O'Malley 2008).

From and economic standpoint neo-liberalism has five basic characteristics. First, liberating "free" enterprise or private enterprise from any sanctions imposed by the government regardless of the social damage this causes such as, a greater openness to international trade and investment (North American Free Trade Agreement). Other examples are decreased wages, union busting, and getting rid of workers' rights that had been fought for over many years of struggle. Eliminate price controls, total freedom of movement for capital, goods and services. They contend that an unhindered market is the best way to prosper the economy, which in the end will benefit everyone. It's like Reagan's "supply-side" and "trickle-down" economics -- but unfortunately the wealth didn't trickle down (Martinez and Garcia, 2000).

Second is decreasing public spending for social services for the economically disadvantaged and even maintenance of highways, bridges, water supply -- again in the name of eliminating government's role. However, they don't oppose government subsidies and tax breaks for business. Third is deregulation, decrease government regulation of everything that could hinder profits, including protecting the environment and workplace safety. Next is privatization, which is to auction off state-owned enterprises, goods and services to private investors such as banks, certain industries, railroads, toll ways, utilities, schools, hospitals and even fresh water. Although usually done in the name of greater efficiency, which is frequently needed, outsourcing has mainly had the effect of concentrating money even more in a few hands and making the public pay even more for its needs. Last are eliminating the idea of the public good and community and focusing on "individual responsibility," forcing the poorest people in society to come up with solutions to their lack of medical care, education and social security all by themselves – then pointing the finger at them if they fail (Martinez and Garcia, 2000).

Welfare to Work or Welfare to Prison? Bill Clinton and the Neo Democrats

In 1992 as the nation's public aid caseload reached 13.6 million citizens, Bill Clinton campaigned for the presidency and led the charge for the demise of welfare as we know it (Shaw 2007). The demonizing of the poor was epitomized by the 1996 welfare policies of Bill Clinton's administration. The neoliberal movement, as well as critics of public aid, grew exponentially. President William Jefferson Clinton, a liberal, authorized the Personal Responsibility and Work Opportunity Reconciliation Act of 1996 (commonly known as the Welfare Reform Act), legislation passed by the conservative-controlled Congress. The law stopped some federal welfare programs, put permanent limits on the money utilized for federal welfare funding, and handed every state a block grant to assist in running its own welfare programs. The legislation also tells each state government to come up with a new welfare strategy that meets new federal standards. Under the 1996 legislation, federal monies can be utilized to provide a total of just five years of assistance in an entire lifespan for a family (Alexander 2010; Shaw 2007; Ismaili 2006). Under his tenure there was a restoration of the correctional state that looked to handle the crisis of the unanticipated social consequences of this. In other words, as opportunities for employment and welfare assistance shrank, crime was increasingly a more tempting option, which fostered increasing amounts of imprisonment as well as a growth of the penal state. This represented a reforming of social welfare and correctional legislation (Wacquant 2010; Campbell 2010; Wacquant 1998).

To the societal extent we witnessed the implementation of increased law-and-order perversion, which has involved the growing representation of penal activity in the news media and Hollywood for the main goal of being shown in a ritualized manner, presumably to let the public know the sanctions connected to crime. In short, we observed the double regulation of the poor through the marriage of social and criminal justice policy at the lower end of an increasingly polarized class structure—a major structural innovation very apparent in America, also taking root in every industrialized nation that has bent to the fierce pressure to fall in line with American neo-liberalism (Wacquant 2010; Campbell 2010; Wacquant 1998).

Three Strikes and Minimum Mandatories

Neo-liberalism, like neo-conservatism, took a swing at reforming welfare and had its hand in supporting tougher sentencing, anticrime and antidrug laws that disproportionately targeted the poor and minorities. For example, Democrats started competing with Republicans to show that they could be even tougher on the dark-colored parasites. The policy of correctional growth is not just a Republican agenda. Under his tenure, President Bill Clinton declared how proud he was to put an end to "big government"; and the commission for reform of the federal state, run by his would-be successor, Al Gore, had been busy cutting public-sector services and employment. In the meantime, 213 new correctional facilities had been erected (Alexander 2010; Wacquant 1998).

President Clinton stated, "I can be scraped a lot, but nobody can say I am easy on crime." The statistics show he is true to his word. Clinton's "tough on crime" legislation created the biggest growth in federal and state correctional inmates of any president in the history of the United States. President Clinton was not content with just growing prison populations. He and the Neo Democrats led the charge in policies restricting drug felons from government housing (no matter how small the crime) and restricting them from basic public aid, including food stamps, for life. Discrimination in almost every area of political, economic, and social life is presently completely legal—if you've been labeled felon. These policies particularly impact minorities. Race is a growing issue impacting the welfare discussion because one can't ignore the inequality of wealth amongst race lines; for example, statistics in the (2000) US Census Bureau study showed that the median household net worth for Caucasians was $75,000; on the other hand, for African American families it was about $7,500 (Alexander 2010; Shaw 2007).

All that Glitters Is Not Gold

Attorney General Eric Holder recently announced that the United States Department of Justice would cease seeking lengthy mandatory minimum sentences in some federal drug prosecutions. He concurrently issued a memorandum directing federal prosecutors on the new legislation. But what does the legislation really mean, and in what manner will it affect federal drug prosecutions? In practice, the legislation dramatically enhances the power and discretion of federal prosecutors, while giving an opportunity for some defendants to escape severe mandatory minimum sentences. The Holder Memorandum implies taking this more lenient step when the following requirements are met: (1) the accused conduct doesn't involve violence or trafficking to minors, (2) the individual is not a leader of others in criminal actions, (3) the defendant does not have "significant connections" to large-scale drug-trafficking organizations, and (4) the individual doesn't have a "significant" criminal background, with "significant" meaning roughly three criminal history points under the guidelines. The problem is it is extremely easy to get more than three criminal history points. It's especially easy if you're economically disadvantaged. Criminal history calculations are driven in part by the sentence you served on the prior. If you're indigent, and you get charged with something relatively small, you most likely didn't get bail; and you more than likely plea-bargained out to time served after a few months of hassle. If you're rich, you most likely got bail and pled you receive probation. If you received a sentence of sixty days, you get two criminal history hits; if you received probation you receive one. In short, the Holder Memorandum directs prosecutors to prevent application of mandatory minimum sentences for a select group of less-culpable defendants (Popehat 2013).

While the nation appears to be reforming strict laws, it still has not addressed the issue of three-strikes-and-you-are-out laws as well as the defunding of state psychiatric hospitals, which are two of the other major players in prison overcrowding. These issues must be addressed—hiding our heads in the sand and pretending it is not a problem is not just ignorant but also immoral. We can turn a blind eye to the fact that too many mentally ill patients wind up in prison, but what are we going to do when those individuals are preyed on and victimized in jail, which is what happens to many of the mentally ill, and then after several years are released back into mainstream society?

Neo-Cons Rising and The Contract With or (on) America?

Economic and social instability of the 1960s and 1970s produced a backlash against both the perceived incompetence of the welfare system and the permissive/

selfish culture that was supposedly subverting society. While a political movement against Keynesian economics and moral individualism had been in existence in America as early as the 1960s, it was in the 1970s and 1980s that it generated more influence. Crime became a big issue in the political debate of the 1980s and was largely due to neoconservative politics that brought this issue to the forefront of British and American political campaigns. It was this political environment that helped subvert the rehabilitative philosophy and made it possible to build the criminal issue as a social-control issue instead of a public-health/ socioeconomic issue. Under the sway of neoconservative methods to criminal justice and public safety, citizens are prodded to view crime as an inevitable risk of contemporary life and to submit to ever more aggressive methods of law enforcement, private policing, and punishment. The ideology is not just to fight crime but to manage its threats, to instill personal vigilance in the people, and to incorporate criminals' knowledge via informants and obtaining intelligence. In 1988, at the prompting of the National Governors Association and Ronald Reagan, the US House of Representatives created the Family Support Act, which put in place the initial targets for putting public aid recipients to work. The neoconservative movement under Ronald Reagan and the contemporary suburban middle class grew to see bureaucracies and the welfare state as massive drains on government budgets (Wacquant 1999; Change Lab 2012).

Political leaders like Thatcher, Reagan, and Bush were not only motivated by the ideological desire to shape an unhindered marketplace, but they also held a deep disdain toward a society that had, from their perspective, become excessively permissive, unruly, and dependent on welfare. In this bond of free-market liberalism and neoconservative authoritarianism, the *New Right* had been birthed. Neoconservatives dedicated themselves to welfare reform and getting "Tough on Crime." These policies disproportionately affected the poor and minorities. These neoconservative policies created a "prison house of nations" that saw correctional populations explode to the point where America houses one-fifth of the world's prison population (Ismaili 2006; Clear, Cole, and Reiseg 2010). Then in 1996 Bill Clinton implemented sweeping and punitive transformations to welfare legislation. In doing this, he followed through with one of the central objectives of the Contract with America. This was the conservative philosophy pushed by Newt Gingrich during the 1994 congressional elections, midway through Clinton's initial term. The policy concepts it contained were generated from the Heritage Foundation, one of the most prominent right-wing think tanks (Wacquant 1999; Change Lab 2012).

How did a liberal president wind up implementing neoconservative policy? That's the power of neoconservative movements. Over the previous half-century they have successfully steered the political paradigm further and further to the right so much that Clinton and Obama have enacted legislation that are securely a component of right-wing philosophy. The tactic behind the Contract with America ended up bringing in a Republican majority in the House and Senate in 1994 for the first time in almost a half-century, by feeding on Caucasian racial bitterness. Similar to the Southern tactic of the 1960s that appealed to racism to switch the South from liberal to conservative, the Contract with America depended on the perception that government services like welfare aided African Americans at the expense of a backsliding Caucasian middle class. Clinton's implementation of welfare reform mirrored this rightward drift that has taken a massive toll on neighborhoods of color both in America and the Global South. He also enlarged the correctional system, implemented destructive free-trade legislation, and created the most severe immigration legislation since the time of exclusion acts. Conservative cries for limited government, however, do not apply to correctional facilities with the yearly payroll for prisons now past $10 billion (Wacquant 1999; Change Lab 2012).

Penalizing the Poor

The American criminal justice system has historically disproportionately targeted the poor and minorities. And under neoliberal and neoconservative practices it continues to do so. This is very evident to see when one looks at the landscape and demographics of those being held in correctional facilities. Looking at the criminal justice terrain, it is also clear that the rich and powerful usually manage to elude prison. The fact that this happens is no accident. The War on Drugs, three-strikes-and-you're-out laws, as well as minimum mandatory sentencing all helped perpetuate the mass incarceration of the indigent and minorities, particularly African Americans. According to Maria McFarland, deputy director for the US Program of Human Rights Watch, this is one of the big human rights issues in America. Many of the people tangled in the criminal justice system are economically disadvantaged and racial and ethnic minorities frequently thrown away by society. Neo-conservatism anticrime control legislation as much as neo-liberalism has contributed to injustice and mass imprisonment. Neoconservative doctrine actually exacerbates the very conditions resulting in criminal activity in the first place. America's most prominent modern economist say that within America's neoconservative criminal justice system, incarceration frequently becomes a breeding ground for countercultural identity, particularly the breeding ground for future crime (Biron 2013; Zafirovski 2008).

Under neoconservative doctrine there has been an unparalleled and unrivaled growth of correctional facilities in the United States since the 1980s, with most growth in the South and western regions, such as Texas, Florida, Virginia, and even California, under neo-conservatism (Zafirovski 2008). For example, California, is supposed to be liberal; however, the states' corrections spending was frequently more than money allocated for education (Bordieu 1998) according to a nonpartisan public policy group called California Common Sense, whose study, Winners and Losers: Corrections and Higher Education in California, looked at the state's general fund expenditures on corrections and higher education from the period between 1981 and 2011 (Anand 2012; Zafirovski 2008).

American taxpayers have seen a "correctional explosion." Prison overcrowding surpassed prison construction budgets, and politicians who had promised to build new prisons could no longer build them. So in 1984, a number of Tennessee investors with close friends in the legislature recognized a business opportunity and formed Corrections Corporation of America (CCA). Their plan was to use venture capital to build a new prison and—like a hotel—lease their beds to the state in a profit-making endeavor (Corrections Project 2013).

Currently, almost 10 percent of American correctional facilities and jails (meaning two hundred thousand prisoners) have been privatized, the three biggest being CCA, Wackenhut Corrections Corporation, and Cornell Corrections Inc. The US government also contracts with them to house an expanding amount of undocumented immigrants and resident aliens, while some of the private prisons have facilities in nations outside America. Correctional Corporations have accumulated vast political power through government connections, lobbying power and campaign contributions, while attempting to transform the discourse of justice into the language of the marketplace. In this manner, they imply government agencies have a stranglehold on corrections, push the need to downsize, and cut through red tape. They posit that they can operate correctional facilities more efficiently and at a lower price, performing a more efficient job and saving the citizens tax dollars (Corrections Project 2013).

Elitist Criminal Justice Policies

The American judicial system focuses moral condemnation on people and steers it away from the social order that may have either violated the person's rights or dignity or basically pushed them to the brink of the crime. This not only serves to sound the call that our social institutions are not in need of basic questioning, but it also further implies that the justice of our institutions is clear, not to be doubted. Not only does the criminal justice system exonerate the social chain of command of any indictment of injustice, but it also intentionally hides the society's own criminogenic tendencies by pointing the finger at an individual for a crime. Our culture is cleared of the charge of complicity in the wrongdoing. Even more damaging, by punishing mainly the indigent, we overlook the wrongdoing of the rich. White collar criminals who take millions of dollars are regularly let go after minimal prison sentences of a few months or a few years at most, while the underprivileged are put away for years at a time for nonviolent drug crimes and property crimes. The average prison sentence for savings and loan offenders from 1988 to 1992 was three years; the average prison term for burglary is 56 months, and 38 months for automobile theft. The average loss in a savings and loan case is half a million dollars. The average loss for property offense in the mid-1990s was $1,251. At the beginning of the decade, the sum cost of white-collar crime was $404 *billion.* The sum amount taken in all property crimes reported in 2000 was $16 billion. However, corporate executives hardly ever end up in prison (Reiman and Leighton 2010).

David Cole, constitutional law scholar, civil liberties advocate, and author of *No Equal Justice,* examined race and class double standards in criminal justice and looked at the basic inequalities in the American legal system. Cole (1999) examines subjects varying from law enforcement behavior and jury selection to sentencing and posits that our system fails to live up to the promise of equality but actively requires double standards to function. Such disparities, Cole contends, permit the elite to enjoy constitutional safeguards from law enforcement power without paying the price associated with extending those protections across the board to minorities and the poor.

Although overt discrimination has diminished some in the criminal justice system over recent decades, at the beginning of the twenty-first century, we continue to grapple with the perceptions and the reality of unfairness in our justice system. Racial and ethnic disparities persist in crime and criminal justice in the United States. Minorities remain overrepresented in delinquency, offending, victimization, and at all stages of the criminal justice process from arrest to pretrial detention, sentencing (including capital punishment), and confinement. Minorities, particularly African Americans, are generally overrepresented in the criminal justice system both as offenders and as victims, and the rate of black women under control of the criminal justice system is growing faster than for any other group, including black men and white men (Rosich 2007).

The bail system fosters conditions that raise the chances for detention of underprivileged defendants, and the freedom of prosecutors to charge them with a crime is a potent weapon that can lead to inequality. Many poor people have to settle for plea deals; many poor citizens do not have the money to post bail because they have to utilize their scarce resources for food, utilities, rent, etc. For minorities and the economically disadvantaged, plea bargaining is a system that is best defined as condemnation without adjudication. A method that takes the place of a trial (which is what our Constitution intended) with plea deals. Many times, those deals utilize coercion (Langbein 2004). The DA is basically pressuring individuals to surrender their rights to jury trial, sometimes intimidating them with even more sanctions if they resist the plea deal and ask for the right to jury trial. The plain reality is there is not a bunch of Rockefellers in prison for robbing convenient stores or drug trafficking. The majority of people trapped in the criminal justice system, for all kinds of sad reasons, is individuals who are underprivileged. When you combine pretrial detention with the prosecutor's ability to coerce greater sanctions if a person does not confess and bear false witness against themselves, many people trapped in that scenario basically have no option but to bear false witness against themselves and confess to crimes they did not commit. Over the previous three decades, the most damaging results of criminal justice legislation and practices have been aimed at enormous levels toward young black males from urban areas, the economically disadvantaged, and those in economically deprived communities (Langbein 2004; Rosich 2007).

America has taken great strides over the past fifty years toward the goal of making sure there is equality under law for all citizens. However, in the criminal justice mechanism, racial inequality is expanding, not declining. To handle the crime problem and deter criminals, US society utilizes formal social controls, namely the criminal justice system. Unfortunately, the chances of being arrested, convicted, and sentenced seem to be clearly linked to money and social class. Criminal legislation, while cosmetically neutral, is enforced in ways that are vastly and pervasively prejudiced. In America, our criminal justice system has gone far off course of the noble idea of equal justice for all. African Americans, Latinos, and other minorities are being assaulted by disproportionate targeting and unfair treatment by law enforcement, police officials through racially distorted booking, plea-bargaining decisions of Das, biased sentencing procedures, the lack of effort of the judicial sector, politicians, and other criminal justice legislators to fix the injustices (Uggen and Wheelock 2006; Weich and Angulo 2000).

For most well-to-do, wealthy people, the experience of imprisonment is a mere brush, experienced after a child's arrest. For a vast number of indigent people in America, especially underprivileged African American men, imprisonment is a journey that braids through an ordinary life, much like high school and higher education do for wealthy kids. More than 50 percent of all black men without a high-school education end up in correctional facilities at some period in their lives (Gopnik 2012).

Mass imprisonment on a level virtually unparalleled in human history is a basic fact of our country today—maybe the basic fact, as slavery was the basic fact of 1850. In reality, there are more black males in the grasp of the judicial system—in prison, on probation, or on parole—than were enslaved then. In total, there are presently more people under correctional supervision in the United States than were in the Gulag under Stalin at its peak. The magnitude and the harshness of our prisons are the moral debacle of American life. Each day, at least fifty thousand men—a full stadium at soldier field—wake in solitary confinement, frequently in super-max prisons or prison sections, in which men are detained in tiny cells, where they can see nobody, can't freely read a book or write a letter or poem, and are only permitted out merely once a day for sixty minutes solo "exercise." Enclose yourself in your bathroom and then visualize you have to stay there for the next decade, and you will have some idea of the experience. Prison rape is so rampant—more than seventy thousand inmates are sexually violated every year—that it is regularly held out as a threat, an aspect of the punishment to be expected. The topic is regular fodder for comedy, and an uncooperative suspect being threatened with rape in prison is now represented every day on television, as a regular and rather admirable piece of policing. The normalization of correctional rape like eighteenth-century chat about seeing people fight for their lives as they perish in the gallows will absolutely strike our forefathers as disturbingly sadistic, unimaginable on the part of people who perceived themselves to be civil (Gopnik 2012).

Arrest. The weeding out of the rich often initiates at the arrest but happens mainly via legislation. Government documents, including numerous amounts of research, address the inequality apparent in official records and self-report. While African Americans and Caucasians admit to similar amounts and kinds of law breaking, it is the indigent that have a greater chance of being arrested and obtaining a criminal record. Some researchers contend that at the start of the path to prison, law enforcement primarily investigates and arrests individuals that have the least political influence or who are least likely to bring attention to law enforcement practices. Those are typically people in the lower social and economic categories, i.e., minorities and poor whites (Reiman and Leighton 2013).

Conviction

The most seminal occurrence in the criminal justice system in our era was the trial and exoneration of O. J. Simpson in Los Angeles for the alleged killing of his former wife and her associate Ron Goldman. Regardless of Simpson's guilt or innocence, the case clearly demonstrated that class wins over race more when it comes to the criminal justice system. At every phase of the case Simpson was able to get preferential treatment and outcomes. This varied from the very apparent (the "dream team" of legal counsel who represented him) to the subtle (the DA's decision not to seek the death penalty.) The question of guilt or innocence is dramatically impacted by one's ability to obtain the money needed to be free on bail and secure legal representation other than a court-appointed attorney. Both require the ability to obtain finances, and because of this, the economically disadvantaged are more likely to be convicted. Those who are not employed are three times more likely to be jailed before trial than those who are working, and people who cannot make bail have a greater chance of being convicted. There are distinct benefits to the legal services money can obtain, particularly in capital murder cases (Wright 2013; Reiman and Leighton 2013).

Sentencing

Considerable evidence exists from a large body of empirical research that race and ethnicity do play a role in contemporary sentencing practices. For example, studies have looked into whether minority defendants are at a disadvantage at the pretrial phase of the judicial system. Results show that court-appointed attorneys or other services established by states to give counsel for poor defendants (a vast number of whom are minorities) do not provide the quality of legal aid enjoyed by those who can afford to pay for legal representation. The harshest sentences are dished out to lower-class defendants while the upper crust of criminals avoids incarceration or gets a more lenient sentence. For example, white-collar crime like the savings and loan scandal cost American citizens billions of dollars. However, those executives convicted got less prison time than poor people convicted of common property crimes. Huge violations of trust and power, like those involved in Watergate and corporate crime, are hardly ever the subject of "get tough" laws and are dealt with leniently (Reihman and Leighton 2013; Rosich 2007).

Class in America is almost a taboo subject. Bring the topic up in any context—no matter if it is tax policy, campaign finance, government subsidies to corporations, and criminal justice—and the person is expediently dismissed as a maniac or, worse, of instigating a class war. Forget that the class war is already being fought on the underprivileged and the criminal justice apparatus is the weapon of choice in this war. Class lurks like an elephant in a swimming pool where all the dinner guests are too nice to discuss its existence. Ignoring the role that class plays in the criminal justice apparatus, and politics in general, makes it just about impossible to deal with the root cause of the large amounts of people incarcerated in America (Wright 2013).

While Americans may feel nostalgia for a golden age of small towns and strong communities, the past illustrates a less noble view of the criminal justice system. The rich and powerful have received leniency when they commit crimes, yet the poor are dealt with in an excessively harsh manner. Throughout history, US criminal justice has favored the rich over the underprivileged. Reiman and Leighton (2010) examined the methods in which American correctional facilities come to be mostly filled with people in the underprivileged sections of society. They contend that the judicial system does little to stop numerous harmful acts done by the elite and that the judicial system actually forms a protective barrier around the rich while simultaneously operating in a manner where the economically disadvantaged have a greater chance of being arrested, being booked, are at an increased chance to be convicted, and have an increased chance of being given lengthier prison sentences (Sherman 2001; Reiman and Leighton 2010).

Reiman and Leighton's *The Rich Get Rich and The Poor Get Prison* (2012) also contend that refusal to make workplaces safe, unwillingness to decrease deadly pollution, fostering of unneeded medical procedures, and prescriptions for unneeded pharmaceuticals do as much damage as the misdeeds of the economically disadvantaged. However, the misdeeds of the wealthy are virtually never dealt with as criminal, and the times when they are, they are never dealt with as harshly as the misdeeds of the lower class. The criminal justice system not only refuses to safeguard society against the dangerous acts of the rich and powerful, but it is also incompetent in remedying the reasons for street crime, like poverty, which causes a large population of poor people to be imprisoned (Sherman 2001; Gottschalk 2012; Reiman and Leighton 2012).

It has been stated that the United States has the best justice system that money can purchase. For the most part, the clear dishonest actions of third-world banana republics, with money transferring hands for exoneration or the dismissal of prosecutions is not present in the United States. Instead, the dishonesty is more subtle and much worse: the system is biased. In a banana republic, a dishonest judge or DA is neutral to the degree that they pimp their services to the highest bidder. The class-biased judge or DA, by comparison, is the legal equivalent of going to Atlantic City, where the odds inherently favor the house and most likely won't change. The most apparent difference with rich criminals is that they can pay for the best criminal defense attorneys, private investigators, and expert witnesses. The state has almost unlimited budgets to investigate and prosecute those crimes it decides to go after. A poor defendant with a public defender with no resources for expert witnesses or investigators is just being "processed" through the courts and into jail. It is calculated that O. J. Simpson utilized between \$3 and $5 million on his attorneys. That is what it takes to make the playing field level in a serious criminal case. It is also past the grasp of all but the richest of criminal defendants (Wright 2013).

Disparities/ Inequality in Sentencing

Laws. There is a triple bias against the economically disadvantaged. First, laws are made in a manner that determines what gets labeled a crime and which ones are handled as regulatory issues. The misdeeds of the underprivileged are handled as crimes and those of the rich are viewed as regulatory. Drug legislation is a vital component of the contemporary criminal justice system, as it makes up a massive feeder into the predominantly African American and Latino prison jail population. Crack cocaine became widespread in the middle part of the 1980s and got large amounts of media attention partially because of its massive growth in the drug trade. The popularity of crack cocaine was linked to its affordable price tag, which for the first time made cocaine more accessible to a broader economic class. In the wake of massive news attention, crack was portrayed as a violence-inducing, extremely addictive drug that caused a plethora of social ills, particularly in urban communities. With the media targeting crack, Congress expediently agreed to federal sentencing legislation in 1986 and 1988. This included mandatory sentencing legislation based on the proposition that crack cocaine was fifty times more addictive than powder cocaine. Congress doubled that amount and brought forth a sentencing policy based on the weight of the drug a person was convicted of selling. Federal sentences for crack were built to relate to sentences for powder cocaine in a 100:1 quantity ratio (Barak, Leighton, Flavin 2010; Coyle 2003).

The crossing of racial dynamics with the criminal justice system in America has a long and storied history. In previous generations, courtrooms in many jurisdictions were made up of Caucasian decision makers. In modern society, there is greater diversity of leadership in the judicial system; however, color still plays a vital role in numerous criminal justice outcomes. This includes racially disparate traffic stops, racial profiling, and the administration of capital punishment because of the color of victim or offender. An especially vital component of the role of race in the justice system relates to sentencing. The possibility of a racially discriminatory procedure is opposed to the ideals of fair treatment under law upon which the criminal justice system is founded (Sentencing Project 2005).

Evidence implies that while racial dynamics have transformed over the years, race still has an undeniable presence in sentencing. African American defendants convicted of harming Caucasian victims are given harsher sanctions than African Americans who engage in crimes against other African Americans or Caucasian defendants who harm whites; African American and Hispanic defendants are frequently sentenced more harshly than comparably situated Caucasian defendants for smaller violations of the law, particularly drug and property crimes. When analyzing the federal level, over two-thirds (68.2 percent) of the estimates of the direct effect of color on sentencing point to more severe sentences for African Americans, and 47.6 percent of the estimates of the direct impact of color/race on sentencing registered more severe sanctions for Hispanics (Spohn 2000; Gruehl, Spohn, and Welch 1981).

One government study (Cassia Spohn's 2000 survey of the relevant studies produced for the National Institute of Justice) has concluded that African American and Latino males are more likely to be handed out lengthier prison sentences than their Caucasian contemporaries since the Supreme Court loosened federal sentencing regulations. The research by the US Sentencing Commission refueled a long-standing argument as to whether federal judges should to be held to mandatory guidelines so to eradicate what might be seen as inherent biases and drastically different sentences. The study examined sentences given out since the January 2005 *US v. Booker* decision that allowed federal judges greater sentencing discretion.

The commission discovered that the disparity reached its zenith in 1999 with African Americans being given 14 percent longer sentences. After the *Booker* case, the disparities seem to have grown steadily, with African American men being given sentences up to 10 percent higher than those given to their Caucasian contemporaries. Using another method of analyzing the data, the study found black men received sentences that were 23 percent longer than white men's sentences. Latino males, meanwhile, were given sentences that were about 7 percent lengthier than Caucasian men's sentences. Immigrants also received lengthier sentences than American citizens (Taylor 2010).

Hollywood Law and Order Pornography and Drive by Journalism

Western culture is fascinated with crime and justice. Americans in particular have an obsession with crime and justice. There has become a grand merry-go-round of myth about crime and criminals. Subsequently, the prison-industrial complex has become the thing of our escapist buffooneries. Our culture regards arrests, prosecutions, and incarcerations as foundational props of our mass culture, thus lifting one of the more unpleasant tasks and duties of the civil society, the prosecution and punishment of people who break its laws into a cultural commodity. From movies, books, newspapers, magazines, and television shows, we are continually participating in crime rhetoric. The news media are vital players in the molding of criminality and the criminal justice system. Citizen's view of victims, criminals, deviants, and police officials is mainly decided by their depiction in the news media. Studies indicate that the vast amount of citizens' knowledge about crime and justice is drawn from the news. Therefore, it is critical to analyze the impact that the news media has on attitudes about crime and justice (Dowler 2003). One of the big instigators of the "war on crime" was low-budget television shows, also referred to as drive-by journalism. There is *CSI, Law and Order Special Victims Unit, NYPD Blue*, etc., which fuels the citizens' ever-growing phobia of crime. According to FBI UCS, crime rates in America have actually declined in the same era which ABC, NBC, and CBS have quadrupled the amount of law and order perversion in their evening media programs, usually showing five stories an evening (Wacquant 1999; Dowler, 2003).

Media Depictions of the Underprivileged

Media representation of minorities is very rarely portrayed in a positive manner and the mainstream media implies those who are minorities are inherently different from the rest of us, designing make-believe divisions and differences. The Media Monitoring Committee and its Visual Task Force are citing a study by Yale political scientist Martin Gilens (1999), which says that while most poor people in America are white, most underprivileged people depicted by the national news media are African American. His study of four years' worth of articles from *Time, Newsweek*, and *U.S. News & World Report* discovered that a large percentage of the poor people in their stories were depicted as African Americans. Studies on how blacks are represented on prime-time television from 1955 to 1986 discovered that only 6 percent of the people were African American, while 89 percent of the TV population was Caucasian. Out of these African American characters, 49 percent did not have a high school diploma and 47 percent were poor. Since local news media may be the main venue of learning for many adults, it is a central part in legislative debates with regard to civil rights, the public's basic knowledge about minority communities, and a wider and more complete worldview (Chandler 2011; Butler 2006; Parenti 1992; Lichter 1987; Washington, 2008).

When the latest photos come in of pestilence, natural disaster, disease, or famine, the media reacts quickly and with sensitivity, and money often floods into charities. It is harder to convey the long-running, grinding disadvantage experienced by those who may not be living quite so apparently in economic ruin. Research implies that the news is selective in the subjects it covers; with the plight of kids and the elderly far more likely to be on the news agenda because they are seen as more worthy of our sympathy. Media coverage has a tendency to pigeonhole people, putting them in groups as heroes, victims, or villains. In America, classist stereotypes about the traits and actions of underprivileged people are pervasive. Very few stories about issues surrounding the debate on poverty make it to the mainstream, and when literature about those living in poverty surface, they are frequently negative and have no real substance. The news media has an enormous impact when it comes to how people perceive social class and the different groups within. Particularly because individuals usually reside and socialize with people in their own social class, their perception of others can be substantially framed by the media depictions. Studies have found this to be accurate and have also discovered that the news media has the ability to mold citizen support for policies for public aid (Joseph Rowntree Foundation 2012; Andersen and Taylor 2007; Butler 2006; Bullock, Wyche, and Williams 2001).

There is scarce sympathetic portrayal of underprivileged people, and the media and society at large portray individuals at the lower end of the social structure as being there because of their own bad choices. The flood of stories about abuses of the welfare system can foster the assumption that everyone getting benefits is not only on the dole but also receiving a nice income. News depictions of welfare also tend to over report messages of dependency. Women have a greater chance than their male counterparts to be depicted as dependent, and women who are receiving public aid are labeled as lazy, disinterested in education, and promiscuous. Almost never are welfare activists portrayed as experts; instead, public officials are generally provided the voice of truth. Although there are situations that seem to confirm such prejudices, the benefits system is a safety net to offer a very basic stipend for individuals who would otherwise have little or nothing (Joseph Rowntree Foundation 2012; Andersen and Taylor 2007; Williams 2001; Gillens 1999; Freeman 1997; Bullock, Wyche and Williams 2001; Washington, 2008).

What tends to get overlooked in American society is who is actually getting the most amount of welfare. The answer to that question is the rich through corporate welfare. In 2006 approximately $59 billion was utilized for traditional social welfare services. However, $92 billion was given to corporate subsidies. So the government spent twice as much more on corporate handouts as it did on food stamps and housing assistance in 2006 (Butterfield 2011; Gillum 2012).

If there is one organization that is so large, so wealthy, and so powerful that it should never get a federal dime, who would you name? A short list that might come to mind would include General Motors, ExxonMobil, Microsoft, and a few others. Did you think about Walmart? If so, you get an A-plus. There is no one that is less deserving of federal support than Wal-Mart; however, it received $37 million from the government in the transportation bill. In 2004, Wal-Mart made a $20,000 profit every minute of every day for a total of $10.3 billion dollars on the year (Progress Report 2014; Butterfield 2011; Gillum 2012).

Who Benefits?
Private Prisons

The prison industry complex is one of the most rapidly growing industries in America, and its investors are on Wall Street. One probably already knows how overpopulated and abusive the American correctional system is, and you may or may not be aware that

America has more individuals incarcerated than even China or Russia. In this era of outsourcing, of course, it's no surprise that numerous detention centers are not actually ran by the government but are outsourced to private organizations. But how do prison corporations make more money? By incarcerating more people and by ensuring that recidivism rates stay high. That means, no positive services geared at returning prisoners to society, and advocacy for harsh legislation and sanctions for even non-violent offenses. It means hiring poorly trained employees, and understaffing and doing what the government does only cheaper (Political Gates 2011).

It is evident that certain people are making large amounts of money off the booming business of detaining human beings behind bars. But who are these organizations? Corrections Corporation of America and GEO Group, the two biggest entities that run detention centers in America. When you hear the term "prison-industrial complex," these two groups are a good definition of that. The incarceration of human beings at record levels is a moral and economic failure, particularly in an era when more and more citizens are battling to make ends meet and when state governments are staring down the barrel of enormous fiscal crises. However, mass imprisonment offers a huge windfall for one special interest group—the privatized prisons (Downs 2013; Paleaz 2013; ACLU 2011). The private contracting of inmates for work promotes incentives to incarcerate people. Correctional facilities rely on this income. Corporate stockholders that earn money off inmates work to lobby for longer sentences, in order to enhance their workforce. This multimillion-dollar entity operates its own trade exhibitions, conventions, websites, and mail-order/Internet catalogs. In addition, it has direct advertising campaigns, architecture companies, construction companies, investment houses on Wall Street, plumbing supplies, food supplies, and armed security. Research by the *Left Business Observer* alleged that the federal corrections industry makes every military helmet, ammunition belt, bulletproof protection, identification tag, clothing, tent, bag, and canteen (Downs 2013; Paleaz 2013; ACLU 2011).

In the 1980s, for-profit correctional facilities started obtaining contracts to run entire jails for the first time. Legislators in both parties reacted to prison crowding by outsourcing: the industry expanded by 1,600 percent over two decades ending in 2009. Currently, one out of six federal prisoners is in a for-profit facility, according to ACLU statistics. Industry executives contend their prisons are efficient and needed. Corrections Corporation of America, the biggest private prison company, incarcerates about eighty thousand inmates over sixteen states. CCA says it combines the price savings and innovation of business with the strict procedures and consistent oversight of government. However, numerous independent analysts do not agree with this assessment. After looking at a battery of research on cost and effectiveness in the industry, experts from the University of Utah summarized in a

2007 report that any budget savings appear nominal (Downs 2013; Paleaz 2013; ACLU 2011).

Cutting More than Costs

Whatever the budget savings may be, American citizens do not necessarily benefit when private corrections are operated at a lower cost. In May, the Southern Poverty Law Center and the American Civil Liberties Union filed a suit claiming that a Mississippi private correctional facility is systematically abusing mentally ill patients, including not giving them proper food and medical treatment. Florida, which recently denied a proposal to transfer over twenty state prisons to private prisons, has found that some private correctional facilities cut health-care programs by as much as 50 percent, bringing up concerns about safety and mistreatment. After analyzing those kinds of trade-offs, *The Week* magazine summarized that as terrible as state-run corrections can be, private prisons are a much greater danger, because they exist only to make a profit off of imprisoned people (ACLU 2011; Downs 2013; Paleaz 2013).

The large expansion of the prison population parallels the growth in the private prison industry, which started in 1984 when Corrections Corporation of America (CCA) was given its first contract to administer a correctional facility in Hamilton County, Tennessee. Since that time private prison corporations have grown to control over 415 state and federal facilities housing over

130,000 prisoners. Similar to the military and biotech industries, the prison industry has utilized lobbying and political campaign donations to promote its own growth and profit. The top main prison corporations, CCA and GEO Group, gave over $2.2 million to state political campaigns in 2010. These institutions have also been successful at placing their own attorneys and lobbyists in state offices where *law and order* legislation were being considered. For instance, Arizona governor Jan Brewer's deputy chief of staff, Paul Senseman, is a former lobbyist for CCA who assisted in drafting the state's notorious anti-immigration legislation that exponentially increased Arizona's imprisonment rates (and CCA's profits) (Occucards 2014).

While private corrections may try to portray themselves as just meeting the current need for prison beds and responding to present market conditions, the truth is, they have worked diligently over the last ten years to create markets for their services. As revenues of private prison companies have expanded over the past decade, the organizations have had greater resources with which to build political power, and they have utilized this power to foster policies that lead to greater rates of imprisonment. For-profit private prisons mainly utilize a three-pronged attack to influence legislation: lobbying, direct campaign contributions, and fostering relationships, networks, and associations (Ashton 2011).

Among members of Congress, the two alleged benefactors of contributions from CCA are its home-state senators, Lamar Alexander and Bob Corker of Tennessee. The Republican legislators, each of whom has allegedly gotten more than $50,000 from CCA according to information compiled by the Sunlight Foundation, represent critical swing votes for pushing reform legislation through the Senate. Another main CCA recipient is allegedly Arizona Republican John McCain, who has reportedly received $32,146 from CCA and is a member of the bipartisan "Gang of Eight" that is laboring to draft legislation. His fellow Gang of Eight member, Marco Rubio, ranks among the top alleged benefactors of money from the Florida-operated GEO Group, receiving $27,300 in contributions over the course of his career. Each of these senators has sponsored legislation that would have enhanced the detention and imprisonment of illegal aliens. Policy by Alexander in 2009, for instance, would have provided for "increased illegal immigrant detention facilities." A bill cosponsored by McCain and Rubio would seek to enhance Operation Streamline, a federal enforcement program that makes illegal entry a crime in certain jurisdictions. There are also those individuals who are on the actual payroll of these corporations, for example Manny Aragon, the New Mexico lawmaker who Wackenhut hired as a lobbyist for New Mexico when they were attempting to start privatization in that state (Ashton 2011).

From Texaswatchdog.org:

Two state legislators from South Texas allegedly have financial connections to a private prison firm that operates facilities for the Texas state prison system—in an era when legislators are debating dramatic new measures to tighten down on corrections companies. State senator Judith Zaffirini, D-Laredo, and state representative Rene Oliveira, D-Brownsville, have alleged financial connections to the private prison organization GEO Group, a Florida-based operation that runs nineteen prisons in Texas, including nine under contract for the Texas Department of Criminal Justice. Zaffirini's husband, Carlos, is an attorney and ally for the firm, previously known as Wackenhut (Political Gates 2012).

Henri Wedell

The person who's invested the most in private prisons is Henri Wedell, who began working on CCA's board of directors in 2000, when the company was dealing with scandals related to inmate abuse and mismanagement. Currently he has over 650,000 shares in CCA that is much more successful these days. Those shares are reported to be worth more than $25 million (Downs 2013).

George Zoley

Another alleged private corrections profiteer who presumably has no ethical problems about the business is George Zoley, the CEO of GEO Group and the second-largest investor in the correctional industry. In fact, he's so proud of his business—which has allegedly committed a huge list of human rights violations—he attempted to get a college football stadium named after it. Zoley netted almost $6 million in 2013 through salary and bonuses alone, but the real money is in stocks—he reportedly holds over 500,000 shares in GEO, and he has made $23 million in stock trades during a year-and-a-half cycle. But you cannot say he has not earned his paycheck, exactly. GEO experienced a 56 percent increase in profits in the initial quarter of 2013, and the company's executives reassured investors that the imprisonment rate wouldn't be going down any time in the near future when announcing its earnings (Downs 2013).

Jeremy Mindich and Matt Sirovich

Both Wedell and Zoley are huge contributors to the Republican Party, but that doesn't mean those on the liberal side of the fence can't play their game. Matt Sirovich and Jeremy Mindich both donate to Democratic legislators and are involved with progressive-leaning organizations like Root Capital, a nonprofit lending company that provides loans to farmers in developing countries to reduce poverty. Their regular occupation, however, is operating Scopia Capital, a hedge fund that is the one of the biggest shareholders of GEO Group (a for-profit prison). The fund holds about $300 million in shares in that company, which represents 12 percent of its whole portfolio. Like Zoley, they are skilled at their craft—their fund outperformed the market by 20 percentage points, and the state of New Jersey retained Scopia to manage $150 million worth of pensions. It should be noted that while being far to the left politically might seem inconsistent with investing in corrections (or managing a hedge fund in the first place), the Democratic Party is completely okay with the imprisonment rate. While Richard Nixon and Ronald Reagan are mainly responsible for the drug-war laws that caused the correctional population to explode, Bill Clinton was a "tough on crime" president who expanded their philosophies. And Vice President Joe Biden was a key player in the Clinton era's crime policies—he crafted the Violent Crime Control and Law Enforcement Act, which, among other things, called for $9.7 billion in increased spending for corrections and harsher penalties for drug offenders (Downs 2013).

Who Suffers? The Casualties of War

A police informant approached Joseph Settembrino about dealing LSD. Settembrino, who was unemployed at the time and needing money to pay his automobile loan, agreed; and while he had never been in trouble with the law, he was given a mandatory ten-year sentence. Brenda Valencia's aunt did not have her driver's license and asked her niece for a ride. Sadly, it was to a home where her aunt dealt seven kilos of cocaine, and while Valencia was completely unaware of the drug trafficking, a cocaine dealer cooperating with the prosecutor's office said she was involved in order to receive a reduced sentence. As a result she received a ten-year sentence and an additional two because her aunt was carrying a concealed weapon in the commission of a felony. On a tip from an informant, law enforcement raided Lance Marrow's residence and discovered narcotics and arrested Marrow and his roommate. The bags that had the crack and cocaine residue belonged to the roommate. Just the dollar bill with cocaine residue belonged to Marrow. Marrow was completely unaware that narcotics were in his residence. Convinced that he was not guilty, Marrow made the decision to go to a jury trial, where at the age of fifty he was found guilty and sentenced to fifteen years to life in prison (Famm 2013).

Minorities

About five out of every one hundred male African Americans are incarcerated, a ratio greater than five times that of their Caucasian counterparts. Over one in three young black males who do not have a high school education are presently incarcerated, and young African American men who quit high school have a greater chance of being imprisoned than in the workforce. Over 50 percent of all black men who do not have a high-school diploma make it into the prison system at some point in their lives. The concentration of imprisonment of young males from poor communities has expanded to the degree that it is now an almost-taken-for-granted occurrence, a situation that impacts families, organizations, businesses, social groups, and interpersonal relationships. Ex-felons are stripped of their voting rights, barred from public assistance and government housing, and is hindered the ability to get a real job. Imprisonment and the consequences connected to it has expanded to the degree that it generates the very social ills on which it feeds. Misguided public sentiment and engrained political interests have molded our crime-prevention legislation. Rather than legislation being built upon solid theory and guided by experts in the field, it has been guided by media sensationalism and political ambition. However, no policy can completely solve the problem of crime, since it arises not simply from the criminal justice system but from deeper social conditions and injustices (Sentencing Project 2010; Clear 2007; Palmer 1999; Western 2005; Pettit 2010; Clear 2009; Bernard and Kurlycheck 1992).

Throughout the twentieth century, African American history has been entangled with America's prisons. African Americans were at a greater risk of going to jail than their white counterparts were, particularly since the 1920s. In order to comprehend why there was a vast expansion of African Americans in the correctional system one must understand what is special about American corrections. Prior to the late 1960s, urban manufacturing facilities aided in guaranteeing the quality of life of low-skilled men in the United States. Urban industry offered not only a decent standard of living but also a daily regiment and a connection to mainstream social institutions. In this vein, deindustrialization was tragic. The resulting pandemic created joblessness in poor inner cities, a bleak economy, a thriving drug trade to promote addiction, and careers in crime (Sentencing Project 2010; Pettit 2010; Clear 2009; Clear 2007; Palmer 1999; Western 2005).

These set of events left those in inner cities, especially young men, susceptible to arrest and prosecution. The prison boom, expanding rapidly at the end of the civil rights movement, produced a completely new level of correctional confinement. Incarceration rates soared to staggering levels among young African American males, especially with the undereducated. The corrections growth has targeted young men of color and is especially directed in the communities in which they live. The economic impact of growing prison legislation has had sociopolitical ramifications as well. Mass imprisonment has had a clear impact in economically disadvantaged and minority communities that are unjustly targeted by drug enforcement tactics (Sentencing Project 2010; Pettit 2010; Clear 2009; Clear 2007; Western 2005; Palmer 1999).

The Death Penalty

Capital punishment in America means if you have the capital you can avoid the punishment. —Unknown

The unequal treatment of minorities in the criminal justice system is one of the most serious problems facing America in the twenty-first century. At the beginning of the century, nearly two thousand citizens were asked to share their views about the judicial system in a survey performed by the National Center for State Courts. The survey showed that only 23 percent of the people surveyed have a large amount of trust in the courts of their communities; 52 percent have only minimal trust. The survey showed discontentment with our judicial system—in access to justice, timeliness, independence, accountability, equality, and fairness. The degree of African American dissatisfaction was higher in every category. Sixty-eight percent of African Americans believed they were treated worse than Caucasians, and almost 45 percent of Caucasians surveyed agreed with this perception (Texas Department of Public Safety 2000; Dunnaville 2012).

Vast amounts of empirical evidence seems to imply that minorities and the economically disadvantaged in the United States are subject to disproportionate arrest rates, unbalanced conviction rates, and increased punishment severity. Color, ethnicity, and social class status are an indicator in the outcomes of the numerous phases within the criminal justice process (Dallas Indicator 2013). For example, based on research by the US Attorney General, racial profiling is in fact real, and minority motorists have received more disparate treatment than Caucasian motorists by police agencies in some areas (Dunnaville 2012; Texas Department of Public Safety 2000).

Research on law enforcement–citizen interaction found a large extent of bias because of the color of the suspect (Jackson 1989). More precisely, when interacting with African Americans (in relation to Caucasians), law enforcement has been found to utilize force both more often and more harshly (Geller 1982; Jacobs and O'Brien 1998; Smith 1986), and they are more often aided by police canine units (Campbell et al. 1998). They are dramatically more likely to arrest African American suspects (Danefer and Schutt 1982; Hepburn 1978; Liska and Chamlin 1984 Hindleand 1978).

Faith in the criminal justice apparatus relies heavily on the extent to which the systems function in a method within its own mission statement of justice. Some contend that America has lost legitimacy in the area of criminal justice, and part of the reason is it does not fulfill its written commitment to treatment of defendants in terms of discrimination due to color, ethnicity, class, and gender. The basis for this position is research and evidence pointing to harsher sentencing of African American criminals than their Caucasian contemporaries, particularly in the utilization of the death penalty. In the United States racial and ethnic disparity in the utilization of capital punishment has been done so on a large scale (Allen 2008; Kleck 1981).

It is tempting to pretend that minorities on death row share a fate in no way connected to our own, that our treatment of them sounds no echoes beyond the chambers in which they die. Such an illusion is ultimately corrosive, for the reverberations of injustice are not so easily confined. The destinies of the two races in this country are indissolubly linked together, 'and the way in which we choose those who will die reveals the depth of moral commitment among the living- Justice William Brennan

Race of Prisoners Currently on Death Row

BLACK: 1,371 (41.58%)
HISPANIC: 374 (11.34%)
WHITE: 1,475 (44.74%)
Source: NAACP-LDF "Death Row USA" (January 1, 2009)

Race of Defendants Executed in the United States Since 1976

BLACK: 393 (34.6%)
HISPANIC: 78 (6.87%)
WHITE: 643 (56.6%)
Source: Death Penalty Information Center

Underprivileged Caucasians/ Mountain People

W. E. B. Du Bois implied that even working-class Caucasians benefited from the wages of membership in a dominant race. However, there is more to the story of class in white America than superiority. The difficulty and success of upward mobility has generated a myth about Caucasian American class structure that clouds the truth. Statistics by the US Census Bureau show that about twenty-two million white people are living in poverty. There is a direct correlation between poverty and criminality; and people living in poverty, therefore, have a far greater propensity for committing property crime, subsequently ending up in the judicial system (Bodnar 2012; Kelly 2000). Placing individuals in jail in America has become the country's biggest program for the underprivileged. Federal, state, and local corrections administrations employ almost 750,000. This makes it the United States' fourth largest employer, behind Walmart and slightly ahead of GM (Wacquant 1999).

Social scientists have long documented the link between systems of punishment and economic structure. In *Capital*, Karl Marx (1867) describes the fate of the industrial reserve. He hypothesizes that class status and economic processes are vital determinants of crime and punishment. Research by Georg Rusche and Otto Kirchheimer (1939), Richard Quinney (1980), and Jeffrey Reiman (2004) are harmonious with Marx's thesis. Punishment under capitalism, these experts contend, mirrors the needs and interests of the elite/ ruling class (Chandler and Austin 2004). The reality is, in the United States, there are two forms of criminal justice, one that exists for the wealthy and a completely different one for the poor. For the wealthy there are kid-glove investigations, lax prosecutions, substance abuse treatment, decreased sentences, and leniency if there is any time in jail. For the economically disadvantaged, however, theirs is one of paramilitary law enforcement, harsh prosecution, strict mandatory sentences, and correctional facilities. Money and the power inherent to wealth, not just color or ethnicity, are the deciding factors in determining which justice system a person will receive (Reiman and Leighton 2010).

In America today, there are more inmates than farmers. And while most prisoners in America are from urban communities, most prisons are now in rural areas providing jobs to those economically disadvantaged areas. During the last two decades, the large-scale use of incarceration to solve social problems has combined with the fallout of globalization to produce an ominous trend: prisons have become a "growth industry" in rural America. Communities plagued by a drop in agricultural, mining, timberwork, and industrial business are now pleading for correctional facilities to be erected in their front yards. The economic reshaping that started in the troubled era of the 1980s has had drastic social and economic consequences for rural areas and small towns. The farm crisis, factories shutting down, corporate downsizing, a move to service sector employment, and the substitution of large regional and national chains for local, main-street businesses have triggered drastic transformations in these areas. The obtaining of correctional facilities as a rational economic development strategy for depressed rural areas and small towns in America has become a pandemic (Mauer and Meda 2002).

Poor Appalachians live precarious lives in unstable, unpredictable communities vulnerable to individual setbacks, such as job loss, illness of a family member, a broken-down car, as well as to the pervasive arbitrary control of those in power and the lack of money to afford legal counsel when arrested. Much like their poor black counterparts, this lack of life's necessities prompts many poor Caucasians to embark in crime. As a result of welfare reform, get-tough legislation and harsh drug laws, underprivileged Caucasian Americans are also targets of mass incarceration. Many whites, most of them indigent and lacking education, are now incarcerated. One-third of America's inmates are Caucasian, and imprisonment rates have grown steadily. Those white inmates are sometimes subjected to incomprehensible mistreatment. While Michelle Alexander (2010) summarizes in *The New Jim Crow: Mass Incarceration in the Age of Colorblindness* that it is no coincidence that the American justice system speeded up its processing of African Americans as the Jim Crow laws enforced since the period of slavery ceased, economically disadvantaged whites are also subjected to this system of social control. If poor whites step on the wrong toes, they will be administered the worst possible treatment and be handled in the same manner as African Americans (Alexander 2010; Wright 2010; Forman 2008; Duncan 1992).

The Mentally Ill

Deinstitutionalization, the closing of state mental hospitals, has been one of the most well-intended but badly planned social evolutions ever carried out in America. It was a result of the overcrowding and deterioration of hospitals, innovative medicine that drastically enhanced the symptoms of about half of patients, and an inability to comprehend that many of the worst patients could not make informed decisions about their own need for medication.

Deinstitutionalization drew enthusiastic support from fiscal conservatives concerned mainly in saving money by closing state hospitals, as well as from civil rights advocates who posited that mental patients needed to be "liberated," as in Ken Kesey's *One Flew Over the Cuckoo's Nest*. This bonding of the political right and left has made for odd—indeed, strange— bedfellows but has been a political juggernaut, making sure that deinstitutionalization will continue to go on, as it does even today, in spite clear proof that for numerous patients it has been a colossal failure.

Using 2004–2005 data not previously published, it was discovered that in America there are over three times more seriously mentally ill people incarcerated than in hospitals. Recent research implies that at least 16 percent of inmates incarcerated have severe psychiatric issues. In 1983 similar research reported that the percentage was 6.4 percent. Thus, in the span of thirty years, the percentage of seriously mentally ill inmates increased threefold. It is now very hard to find a bed for a seriously mentally ill person who needs to be hospitalized. In 1955 there was one psychiatric bed for every three hundred citizens. In 2005 there was one bed for every three thousand citizens. From a historical perspective, we have gone back to the early nineteenth century, when those with psychiatric problems filled correctional facilities. At that time, a revolution, led by Dorothea Dix, fostered more humane treatment of those with psychiatric disorders. For over a century, mentally ill people were treated in hospitals. Our society has now regressed to the conditions of the 1840s by placing vast amounts of mentally ill persons back into jails and prisons (Eslinger et al. 2010).

By the early 1970s, it was very clear that the closing of state mental hospitals had resulted in a dramatic growth in the amount of mentally ill people incarcerated. In 1972 Marc Abramson, a psychiatrist in San Mateo County, published research showing a 36 percent increase in mentally ill inmates in the county jail and a 100 percent growth in mentally ill people determined to be incompetent to stand trial. He also quoted a prison psychiatrist who stated that they were drowning in patients. Many more males are being sent to correctional facilities that have serious psychiatric problems. In 1973 hearings were set up by the California State Senate to talk about the issue. The San Joaquin County sheriff testified that a large amount of psychiatric problems is now being viewed as criminality. In Santa Clara County, the problem of mentally ill prisoners had become ten times larger in comparison to the prior decade (Eslinger et al. 2010).

America's Vulnerable Youth

Our country's juvenile justice systems are set for a foundational, desperately needed change—and not a second too early. Among all of the policy areas impacting fragile children and families, juvenile justice has most likely suffered the most apparent bridge between best practice and common practice, between what we understand and what we most frequently practice. Possibly because it assists an unpopular and powerless element of our society—i.e., emotionally troubled, poor and primarily minority adolescents—juvenile justice legislation has been for too many years molded by bad information, exaggeration, and political bias. The results have been both alarming and come at a high price. Our juvenile justice systems have become tattered with badly conceived strategies that frequently cause and increase crime, endanger our youth and undermine their future prospects, waste billions of citizens' dollars, and subvert our most cherished values concerning equality and justice (Anne Casey Foundation 2008; Chung, Little, and Steinberg 2005; Stier 2009).

These systems impact a broad range of American youth. Nationwide, annually, law enforcement makes 2.2 million juvenile arrests; 1.7 million cases are sent to juvenile courts; approximately 400,000 youths make their way through juvenile detention facilities; and almost 100,000 kids are detained in juvenile correctional facilities, military-style boot camps, and various residential facilities on any given day. Young people who get deeply embedded in the system—those who wind up detained in juvenile centers and training schools—are impacted by some of the worst chances of long-term success of any youth cohort in our country. Over the span of their lives, they will achieve less academically, have less work opportunities, make less money, fail more often to mold enduring families, have increased chronic health problems (including chemical dependency), and suffer greater incarceration rates. If children, as a group, make perfect targets for predators and exploiters, then imprisoned adolescents no doubt make the easiest of that targeted prey. Subject to manipulation and intimidation, with scarce access to legal recourse or independent monitoring and underrepresented in the political system, these kids are easily forgotten by the public. Sadly, the cries from juvenile inmates for the most part goes unheard (Anne Casey Foundation 2008; Chung, Little, and Steinberg 2005; Stier 2009; Political Gates, 2012).

Corruption in the Juvenile Justice System

If it's not the largest scandal in US legal history, many are saying it is at least the lowest point for the nation's troubled juvenile-justice system. Two senior county juvenile-court judges in northeastern Pennsylvania received bribes of $2.6 million in exchange for placing thousands of children off to privately run juvenile facility. Numerous children had committed small offenses and didn't have the benefit of legal counsel. A fourteen-year-old from Wilkes-Barre, for example, spent twelve months in a Glen Mills juvenile facility for the crime of stealing loose change from unlocked cars to purchase potato chips; he was only released after public-interest lawyers fought the constitutionality of the punishment. The miscarriage of justice reaches past the judges, Mark A. Ciavarella Jr. and Michael T. Conahan, who pleaded guilty to federal charges of wire and income tax fraud and who were looking at more than seven years in jail. State and federal authorities continued investigating the case, and the owners of the juvenile facility, PA Child Care, have not yet been charged. The owner, Greg Zappala, stated he was unaware anything illegal or improper was going on, while a former co-owner stated he was victimized by the judges via extortion (Cleland; 2010; Political Gates, 2012).

What's more, many DAs, public defenders, and other judicial officials seemingly looked the other way with regard to the abuses, stunning parents who had expected a fine or probation but instead saw their kids taken off into custody. When the mother of the fourteen-year-old arrested for taking the change asked to retain legal counsel, she was told by one defense counsel it would be a waste of money because the judges would not listen. Now that the plot has been uncovered, some five thousand children have grounds for litigation, and many have already linked up in a class action against the two judges, the center's owner, and other defendants. In addition, many are trying to have their records exonerated; however, their tragic memories of the experience will never go away (Cleland, 2010).

Minority and Underprivileged Women

Female prison populations differ from their male counterparts in several significant ways. First of all, they are less likely to have committed a violent offense and more likely to have been convicted of a crime involving alcohol, other drugs, or property. It is important to point out that in many, property crimes are economically driven, often driven by the abuse/addiction of alcohol and other drugs and or poverty (Covington 1998).

From 1980 through 2010 the number of women incarcerated grew by 646 percent, according to statistics from The Sentencing Project (2005). The number of women incarcerated, a third of whom are imprisoned for drug violations, is growing at almost twice the rate for men. These women frequently have major histories of both physical and sexual abuse, drug abuse, and large rates of HIV infection. Large-scale women's incarceration has resulted in a growing amount of children who face hardship from their mother's imprisonment and the severing of family ties. Judges usually do not take into consideration children when handing out a sentence to a parent. Additionally, women are more likely to have underage kids than men, and grandparents frequently have to take over the parental role and raise their grandchildren. Some children wind up with other family members and possibly in foster care (Buckley 2013).

Another thing to consider is the number of women who are incarcerated who have been abused both sexually and physically prior to being sent to prison. Research released by the Bureau of Justice Statistics in 2007 show that greater than 50 percent of females incarcerated stated that they had been physically or sexually abused prior to their incarceration, in contrast to more than 10 percent of the men. And the amount of substance abuse offenders has grown about 37 percent between 1996 and 2002, representing the greatest source of prison population growth (BJS 2007).

A (1999) study by Miller, Browne, and Maguin discovered that 82 percent of females at New York's Bedford Hills Correctional Facility had a childhood past of severe physical or sexual abuse and that over 90 percent had suffered physical or sexual violence in their lifespan.

Social service professionals imply that traumas from domestic violence and sexual abuses are one of the greatest pathways that lead female victims to a life of addiction. Natalie Sokoloff, a professor of sociology (Women's Research and Judicial Justice) at John Jay College found that women who are imprisoned have a greater tendency to be drug abusers because they have a proclivity to utilize drugs to self-medicate after being abused or experiencing various kinds of violence (Zheng).

While most of the one million women incarcerated in America are for nonviolent offences, many experience severe treatment that advocates say goes against their human rights. For instance, the shackling of female inmates' arms and legs while giving birth remains an often utilized practice in numerous states, according to a human rights organization. Only fourteen states ban the chaining of women while giving birth. However, shackling is not the only treatment that defines many females' experiences in correctional facilities in America. One study discovered that 2.1 percent of women prisoners' experienced sexual misbehavior by a staff member over a ten-month period, and advocates posit the actual number could be much higher. In America, organizations investigating the issue maintain that violence against females in correctional facilities is widespread. Women, who many times suffer sexual abuse and battery in their lives prior to entering correctional facilities, are often re- victimized en masse via systemic violence (Wilson 2011).

Minority/Economically Disadvantaged Children

Approximately two million American children have at least one parent incarcerated, and over 50 percent of the nation's inmates have kids under the age of eighteen. Children whose parents have been arrested and imprisoned have very distinct hardships. Numerous children of incarcerated parents have experienced the emotional pain of instant separation from their primary caregiver, and a vast portion is susceptible to fear, anxiety, anger, sadness, depression and guilt. They may also be moved from caretaker to caretaker (Simmons 2000).

The behavioral consequences are often severe and can result in emotional withdrawal, failure in school, delinquency, and risk of intergenerational incarceration. However, these kids appear to fall through the gaps. Law enforcement does not regularly question at the time of arrest if their prisoners have children; neither do sentencing judges nor correctional institutions frequently pose this question (Parke and Clarke Stewart 2002; Simmons 2000).

Underprivileged to start with, a vast portion of children of the incarcerated become even more underprivileged after their parents' arrest. They display increased rates of anxiety, depression, PTSD, and ADHD. They are at an increased chance of being homeless, having household disruption, educational failure, and delinquency. What becomes of these children? In spite of the vast increase in the number of mothers incarcerated and the possible devastating impact of this imprisonment on future generations, presently, there are only a small amount of prisoner reentry services in America that are specifically targeted to assist whole families affected by imprisonment (Parke and Clarke Stewart 2002; Simmons 2000). This unfortunate scenario only leads to future generations of poverty, hopelessness and incarceration. Children born to imprisoned women in America are typically taken away within three days after birth. In comparison, at Tihar Jail in India, female inmates are permitted to keep their child with them in prison all the way until the child is six years old. When children have a mother or father imprisoned, it causes economic and material hindrances, in addition to creating an imbalance in family relationships and structure. For kids, a parent's imprisonment can result in behavioral and academic problems in school and domestic life. Additionally, it can create social and institutional stigma and embarrassment. Children of incarcerated parents are more vulnerable to depression, anger, and a vast number have signs of posttraumatic stress (Buckley 2013).

Entire Communities

Crime requires punishment, but mass incarceration ultimately punishes the community that the law is supposed to protect. When that community is an economically disadvantaged one boggled down by a history of racial discrimination the rationale to over-punish just to be on the safe side is not just a poor idea but an immoral idea. Prisons separate criminals from their neighborhoods, supposedly leaving those communities safer and stronger. Clear (2007) examined how mass incarceration taken to a radical level, leaves neighborhoods unprotected, the inmate not rehabilitated, and society demonstrably worse off. Clear's position is not that that imprisonment (or the system) is bad, rather, that increased rates of incarceration have unanticipated ramifications. For example, overuse of imprisonment decreases its stigma in indigent inner-city neighborhoods and, subsequently, its deterrent potential (Kennedy and Mika 2001; Clear 2007).

Overuse of corrections also has the impact of taking large amounts of African American dads away from their families and communities, and it diminishes respect for the law in those communities. The notion that imprisonment affects only certain "bad" communities is faulty ideology that results in legislation and perceptions that do not solve the crime problem. This mentality allows for legislation that is not built on solid criminal justice theory but rather by people with limited expertise in the field and politicians who are only motivated by getting elected. When people are taken from their communities and sent to prison in a rural community, that community loses the representation and in turn, loses money calculated in proportion to population. Such communities are frequently home to boarded-up houses, abandoned businesses, and groups of individuals are loitering. High amounts of imprisonment of individuals from economically disadvantaged communities subverts community life, obliterating the most essential foundation of informal social control, and replicates the very components that sustain crime (Clear 2007).

The prison evolution in America has been directed at those most likely to form unstable families, namely the poor and minority men with nominal education. Imprisonment subverts the earning power of men, diminishes their health, erodes family resources, and is a component in the dissolving of families. Additionally, it contributes to the deficits of economically disadvantaged children, solidifying the effects of imprisonment on inequality and passed along to other generations. Having a parent go to prison is now the status quo for economically disadvantaged and minority children. It may raise future racial and class injustice, and potentially foster more crime over the long haul, thereby dismantling any benefits of the correctional boom. American crime legislation has generated families that are more vulnerable and decreased the life chances of youth under the banner of public safety. High American imprisonment is detrimental to later employment, salaries, and family relationships. Because a vast number of incarcerated men are fathers, children are placed at considerable risk by incarceration policies. As imprisonment statistics has skyrocketed, indigent women and children have been left to cope with the separation, visitation, and return of their family. The rapid increase in the research literature unveils how incarceration, on average, negatively affects health. Additionally, it lowers the earnings of adult men, a large number of whom are fathers (Williams 2013; Garfinkel and Western 2011; Western and Wildeman 2010).

Imprisonment also raises the risk of divorce and separation; it decreases the economic resources and quality of life of spouses, and significant others left behind. Additionally, mass imprisonment is tied to social marginalization, behavioral problems and increases in children's aggression. Incarceration lays the groundwork for a vicious cycle, reducing the well-being of fragile families. One in which the criminal justice system does not diminish and may even increase addiction, abuse, and crime (Williams 2013; Western and Wildeman 2010).

Children whose fathers are ex-felons get less financial support than similar children whose fathers haven't been incarcerated. Diminished economic support for children is partially attributed to the extremely limited earning power of formerly incarcerated men, and also to the absence of incarcerated men from their kids' homes (Williams 2013; Garfinkel and Western 2011; Western and Wildeman 2010).

Damage of Governing through Punishment

Social Disenfranchisement

The American prison and punishment apparatus that has ignited since 1970 is a determined and intensely emotional backlash to the promises of the civil rights movement. This apparatus has shamelessly criminalized, stigmatized, and marginalized growing amounts of people who are African American, Latino, poor, mentally ill, young, and now undocumented. The damage is collective, as well as individual. Mass imprisonment and the overuse of harsh punishment on the underprivileged and people of color have stripped them of their power and impoverished entire communities over many generations. In contemporary culture, the resulting, race-founded, rationalizing system to govern through crime has far-reaching implications. Some of the results of drug prosecutions of minor drug offenders have included the right to strip convicted felons of their voting rights permanently. A record number of Americans with criminal records could not vote in the last presidential election. Over 5.85 million adults convicted of a felony are not welcome in the voting booths (Shannon and Uggen 2012; Tucker 2012; Sentencing Project 2012; Glaze 2010; Johnson-Parris 2003).

Punishing individuals with felony records have a detrimental impact on African Americans much more so than other races. For example, 7 percent of African Americans are disenfranchised in contrast to 1.8 percent of the rest of the nation. The amount in Florida and Virginia are much more dramatic; these political battlegrounds were considered vital in determining the results of the election. In Virginia, 20 percent of African Americans are not allowed to vote. In Florida, 23 percent cannot vote. President Obama won Virginia and Florida in 2008 (Shannon and Uggen 2012; Tucker 2012; Sentencing Project 2012; Glaze 2010; Johnson-Parris 2003). When an individual gets labeled a criminal, they are stuck in a vicious cycle that in America is difficult to get out. A permanent record and loss of voting rights are just some of the other consequences of being an ex-felon. More than that is the stigma of being labeled an ex-felon/ex-convict. Individuals who have a criminal record cannot attain a decent job or a decent salary; they are, usually, stuck in a cycle of menial labor and nominal pay or no job at all. Studies do not show a hopeful picture. Research conducted with ex-inmates implies that 60 to 75 percent of the ex-felons stay jobless up to 12 months after release. In light of these statistical results, the fact that 50 percent return to correctional facilities within 36 months is no surprise. Discrimination in almost every area of political, economic, and social life is presently completely legal if you are a felon (Alexander 2010; Recoquillon and Sydenham 2006; Bureau of Justice Statistics 2002).

Other areas of collateral damage have been the destabilization of labor markets, particularly by weakening the earning ability of those who cycle through prisons. In addition, there is a decreased rate of marriage in the African American community, and increased economic pressure on families. Growth in the incarceration of poor and minority women with children is linked to increasing amounts of displaced children and dependents. Drug legislation and overdependence on imprisonment are responsible for growing amounts of chronic unemployment, unstable homes, and increased chance of recidivism (Stevenson *2011; Clear 2009).*

Social Disenfranchisement's Impact on Earning

Garfinkel and Western (2011) unveiled both supply-side and demand-side impact of imprisonment and found that workers may actually be less productive by doing time in correctional facilities and potential employers might be more apprehensive to hire job candidates with criminal records. On the supply side, time imprisoned and separated from the workforce stops inmates from obtaining work experience and occupational skills. Obtaining a job with a prison record has always been a difficult task, but the new dynamics of incarceration extend this issue to nonoffenders as well in African American communities. Given the existence of a prison record, a vast number of employers now assume that almost all African American men have one, hence, the popularity of the criminal background investigation. This causes a real problem for considerations of policy reform to help in reentry. One policy consideration supported by the American Bar Association has been to limit consideration of conviction records unless specifically connected to occupational requirements. Although this appears feasible, a study by economist Harry Holzer (2003) and his associates show how such a tactic might potentially result in even more detrimental effects because of the racist nature of hiring practices. Holzer posited that when employers lack access to criminal records, they have a propensity to believe that almost every African American man must have a record, and, as a result, discriminate against them. Increasingly, legislative policies are being passed to restrict individuals with felonies (especially convictions for drug crimes) from obtaining work, access to welfare benefits, public housing, and eligibility for student loans. These collateral sanctions put up major barriers to a person's social and financial progress (Sentencing Project 2013; Holzer 2003).

Unfair treatment of minorities is a trait of every phase of the process. African Americans, Hispanic Americans, and other minority groups are victimized by disproportionate targeting and unequal treatment by law enforcement and other frontline police officials; via racially skewed charging and plea bargaining decisions of prosecutors. By unfair sentencing practices; and by incompetence of judges, elected officials and other criminal justice lawmakers to fix the injustices (Dunnaville 2012; Greene 1999).

Policy Implications

Five years after the March on Washington DC, Dr. King was vocal against the Vietnam War. Condemning the United States' militarism and imperialism— famously declaring that our country was the largest instigator of violence in the universe. He saw the links between the wars we wage in other countries and the utter apathy we have for underprivileged people and minorities in America. Dr. King perceived the need of openly examining an economic system that will dole out money for war and will put greedy people on a pedestal, but won't give workers a fair living salary. Shortly after the March on Washington, Martin Luther King was ignoring everyone who told him just to stick to discussing civil rights. However, if we as citizens and a nation stay in our lane, we will be overlooking the link between drones abroad and the War on Drugs in this nation. We would also be overlooking the links between the corrupt capitalism that bails out Wall Street, relocates jobs overseas, and forecloses on homes with joy. All while private correctional facilities yield high returns and enhance operations into a new arena: caging immigrants. The most vital lesson we can glean from Dr. King is not what he stated at the March on Washington but what he stated and did after the march. In the time that followed, he did not play political games to see what crumbs a foundationally corrupt system might give to the beggars of justice. Rather, he connected the dots and dedicated himself to establishing a movement that would rock the foundations of our economic and social hierarchy. He did so that the vision he preached on 1963 may one day be a reality for all. He said that nothing short of "a drastic restructuring of society" could give justice and dignity for everyone. He was right. We need to be committed to establishing a movement to dissolve mass imprisonment. However, if all we do is stop mass incarceration, this revolution will not have gone nearly as far as it should. An innovative form of racial and social control will be birthed. Simply because we did not do what King said we should do:

discern the connections between poverty, racism, militarism, and materialism (Alexander 2013).

The policy implications of the last forty years of neoliberal and neoconservative criminal justice legislation have been that of a colossal failure. Reagan's class war directed at labor from 1979 to 1982 saw the average weekly salary drop 8 percent, and between 1980 and 1985, 2.3 million industrial occupations vanished forever. As manufacturing work disappeared, so did retail jobs, the local tax base, and a vast number of municipal jobs (Kraska and Brent 2011; Chadda and Wilson 2011; Vogel 2009). In 1982, the Reagan administration decreased the real value of welfare 24 percent, cut numerous resources for poor kids. His administration also slashed urban development spending, decreased educational block grants, and eliminated the Comprehensive Employment and Training Act that had supplied jobs for hundreds of thousands of people. Reaganomics was an attempt to enhance profit margins by enhancing the rate of exploitation. Even though by the late 1980s, profit margins were rebounding, they were doing so at a huge social price. Chicago saw the amount of people in ghettos expand from the 1980s through 1990s, as well as cities such as Cleveland and Boston. The number of black Americans dislodged into the projects because of the middle-class job exodus expanded dramatically (Kraska and Brent 2011; Chadda and Wilson 2011; Wilson 2010; Giuseppi 2009).

What it did succeed in are a modern era Jim Crow laws that negatively impacted minorities as well as the overrepresentation of the poor. It also succeeded in helping to create a fiscal crisis due to the enormous amount of money needed to sustain the prison-industrial complex. While the prison-industrial complex has become one of the most heavily capitalized areas of the American economy, several failings are very apparent. It has not proven efficient at rehabilitating inmates; it has not decreased crime rates and in fact bears no relationship to crime rates. It has coincided with the most profound increase of violence among young men in the countries existence and pursued incarceration patterns that indicate deeply racist attitudes and policies. In the same way, the military-industrial complex ignited the economic launching of the Reagan/Bush redirection of money and resources. We are seeing the growth of a correctional-industrial complex where taxpayers' already scarce resources and money are taken away from social justice–based methods in favor of incarceration (Hartnett 1997; History is a Weapon 2014).

Future Research

While legislators have focused on crime-fighting initiatives as being key to controlling crime. Research by Bruce Weinberg, coauthor of the study and associate professor of Ohio State University, shows that the impact of labor markets on crime. Politicians can put more police officers on the streets, pass harsher sentencing laws, and take other initiatives to fight crime, but there are limitations to how much these can do. Weinberg's research posits that a poor labor market has a dramatic impact on the crime rates. The thought behind why crime increases in the wake of decreasing wages is simple: a decline in pay increases the relative payoff of criminal activity (Weinberg 2002).

An alternative to imprisonment is any punishment other than time in a correctional facility for individuals who engage in criminal activity. Often, punishments other than prison or jail time put difficult demands on offenders and offer them intensive court and community supervision. Just because a certain punishment does not entail time in corrections does not mean it is easy on crime or is just a slap on the wrist. Alternatives to imprisonment can heal damage suffered by victims, offer benefits to the community, treat the addicted or psychologically ill, and rehabilitate offenders. Alternatives can also decrease correctional costs and hinder additional crimes over the long haul. Before we can optimize the advantages of alternatives to imprisonment. However, we have to undo mandatory minimums and give judges the ability to utilize price-effective, reoffending-reducing sentencing alternatives (Famm 2013).

The Sentencing Project's proposed Racial Impact Statements legislation is one example of utilizing race-conscious mechanisms to pinpoint differential racial effects of criminal justice policies and practices. Reforming three-strikes-and-you're-out, minimum mandatory sentences, as well as harsh drug laws, would go a great length in fixing the wrongs inflicted on the poor, minorities, as well as the pockets of taxpayers. In November of 2012, 70 percent of California's voters were in favor of Proposition 36, which offers changes to the three-strikes-and-you're-out mandatory minimum sentences. Proposition 36 mandates that mandatory minimum life sentences are for third strikes if the crime was serious or a violent felony. The changes were retroactive (Schiraldi and Silva; FAMM 2013).

Media Reform and Better Utilization of Tax Dollars

There is a connection between the troubled assets that were a part of the recent economic crisis and the "troubled assets" of mass imprisonment. The arduous task facing reformers is how to "clear" the complex aggregations of people, social and financial capital, information networks. In addition to the political alliances, and managerial practices generated during the long era in which we increased both the economic and prison bubbles. Support for criminal justice reforms may redirect police and court resources toward more severe crimes, and more effective rehabilitation that have the effect of saving tax dollars for our courts. Numerous states slashed their corrections budgets in 2009, and many suggested shutting down correctional facilities to cover huge budget deficits. States have implemented a myriad of correctional reforms directed at decreasing their penal populations. Additionally, actual corrections and prisoners remain unseen in television news and entertainment. There is a need to open them up to competent media venues so that citizens can see what really goes on in American correctional facilities. (Fox, Sickel, and Steiger 2007; Patchin 2004; Dowler 2003; Abramsky 2002) (Gottschalk 2010; Simon 2010; Sentencing Project 2010).

BJA Justice Reinvestment Initiative, Restorative Justice, and Ban the Box

Justice reinvestment is an information-driven tactic to enhance public safety, decrease corrections and related criminal justice costs and utilizes savings in strategies that can decrease crime and strengthen neighborhoods. It is a tool to fix and restructure the human resources and physical infrastructure of educational facilities, hospitals, parks and public areas of communities devastated by criminal justice legislation. The goal of justice reinvestment is to manage and allocate criminal justice populations price efficiently, producing savings that can be utilized in evidence-based tactics that enhance public safety and holding offenders accountable. Local and State governments participating in justice reinvestment gather and analyze information on things that increase criminal justice populations and costs. Identify and utilize changes to increase efficiencies, and measure both the fiscal and community safety impacts of those changes. In localities as dynamic as Boston, Cincinnati, and Kalamazoo, the resolution is to "Ban the Box." Ban the Box offers ex-felons hope for a fair chance at employment has gained supporters, led mainly by formerly imprisoned people calling for a fair shake. This seemingly small issue has caused an evaluation of our willingness to invoke lifetime punishments by keeping people with criminal records from the workforce (Tucker 2012; Alexander 2010; Lopez 2003; Sentencing Project 2009).

For some time now there has been disillusionment with the justice system. Citizens feel disconnected, victims are unhappy, and those employed in the justice system are bewildered. Legislators are increasingly worried about the growing price of justice in the face of this discord and the high rates of reoffending that exist. Over the last decade, there has been a growing interest in innovative venues to justice that are inclusive of the community and focus on the victim. The modern system where crime is considered an act against the state works on the premise that mainly overlooks and ignores the victim and the neighborhood that is harmed most by crime. The modern form of justice focuses on punishing offenders without making them examine the impact of their crimes. Restorative justice principles provide more inclusive processes and redirect the mission of justice (NIJ 2014).

Restorative justice is on the rise dramatically in America. As citizens continue to experience and see collective "justice" that is jaded racially and economically, by billions in monetary gain, by the warehousing of our meek, an educational-to-correctional pipeline, and by the practices of believing punishment and confinement for all involved when crime occurs to operate as rehabilitative.

There is a revolution in the air, in the political, at the local level, in the hearts of the citizens, which offers a legitimate life ring out of this delusion (NIJ 2014).

Restorative justice is not about overlooking crime or letting people off scot-free. It's not about coercing forgiveness or even about forgiveness per se. It's not about getting rid of important safety considerations from our neighborhoods. Restorative justice may be the most potent solution to the justice mess that we've yet seen. Restorative justice is not a new invention. Utilized for centuries if not more by global indigenous. In New Zealand, it is utilized as the main juvenile justice model. Restorative justice poses the question of who was hurt and looks to fix that harm appropriately. It asks three baseline questions: Who was harmed? What are their needs? Whose obligations are these? (NIJ 2014).

RJ has been finding a receptive audience, because it molds common ground that accommodates the goals of many constituencies and offers a holistic approach. The goals of restorative justice are, crime is an act against human relationships, victims and the communities are vital to justice processes. The number one priority of justice processes is to help victims. The second is to restore the community, to the extent possible that the offender takes personal responsibility to victims and to the neighborhood where the crime happened. Next is that stakeholders share responsibilities for RJ via partnerships for action; and lastly, the offender will gain enhanced competency and comprehension because of the restorative justice experience (NIJ 2014).

Education vs. Incarceration

The United States currently has the dubious distinction of leading the universe in incarceration population: we make up 25 percent of all inmates but only 5 percent of the world population. Our penchant for punishment has been done at a high price. We spend almost $70 billion yearly to put adults in corrections and jails, to detain our children in detention facilities, and to monitor 7.3 million people on probation and parole. Indeed, incarceration costs have claimed a growing amount of state and local government spending. This fad has starved needed social programs, particularly education (Hawkins 2010).

The trade-off between education and incarceration is especially severe at the local level. In many inner-city neighborhoods, where millions of dollars are utilized to incarcerate residents, the education infrastructure is paralyzed. As the corrections population exploded in the last thirty years, experts started to see that large concentrations of prisoners were coming from a few select neighborhoods, particularly indigent communities of color, in large cities. These "million-dollar blocks" mirrored that utilization of tax dollars on incarceration was the predominant public-sector investment in these communities. NAACP (2011) studies reveal that linking zip codes to large rates of imprisonment also reveals where poorly performing schools, as measured by math proficiency, have a proclivity to cluster.

The worst-performing schools have a tendency to be in localities where imprisonment rates are optimal (Hawkins 2010).

California has the biggest correctional population in the nation, with over 170,000 people incarcerated. In Los Angeles, more than 50 percent of current parolees reside in communities that are resident to less than 20 percent of its adult residents. More than a billion dollars are utilized annually to imprison people from these communities. Simultaneously, as of spring 2010, the Los Angeles Unified School District was estimating a deficit of $640 million in the 2010–11 academic years. Because of this, district officials were planning to increase class sizes and give pink slips to thousands of teachers and school-based staff (Hawkins 2010; NAACP 2011).

How is school success impacted by these policy choices and spending cycles? There is no exact way to know what the prior spending cuts have meant for Los Angeles schools. One thing that is concrete is that in Los Angeles, 67 percent of poor-performing schools are in communities with the largest incarceration rates. In comparison, 68 percent of the city's excellent-performing schools are in communities with the lowest imprisonment rates. Cities like Philadelphia and Houston have experienced similar patterns. What we can glean from Los Angeles, Houston, and Philadelphia is that our country's priorities are flawed, and with catastrophic consequences. In a few select communities, a large investment in imprisonment over education correlates with the poorest-performing schools. These communities send more people to correctional facilities than to universities, mirroring the pattern of money invested. The link has yet been shown to be a cause-effect. However; there is a correlative effect between education and incarceration. If states correctly utilized money in reopening schools, maintaining good teachers, keeping proper classroom sizes, and sustaining the affordability of higher education. It's very possible, especially for offenses like low-level drug dealing; there would be no reason to incarcerate so many individuals. Additionally, we could stop putting our valuable taxpayer dollars into an investment that has displayed minimal returns (Hawkins 2010; NAACP 2011).

Discussion and Conclusion

For years, our country has been obsessed with dishing out ever stricter sanctions for crimes big and little. It has done so with little regard as to whether mass incarceration and relegating citizens to a permanent, second-class status hurt or aids the very neighborhoods we claim that we are attempting to help. Maybe the trillion dollars utilized waging the drug could have been more utilized investing in education, job creation, and substance abuse treatment in crime-ridden communities. But regardless, our political leaders have been so zealous to express its authority and control over indigent communities of color that punishment has been the only alternative. It is interesting how we as a nation always appear to have resources for war and prisons, even when the government is cutting spending. It is peculiar how, for decades, we've had a limitless amount of money to erect correctional facilities even as we shut down institutions of learning. Recently, programs like the U.S. Forest Service Job Corps that have been beneficial to economically disadvantaged and minority kids from the inner cities are being downsized. In the meantime, we are pumping more money into the prison system. There's an old statement that when the only thing you have is a hammer, everything appears to be a nail. Desperate individuals here in America and around the globe have come to know that if you plead for help, Uncle Sam comes running with a big hammer swinging in your direction (Alexander 2014).

Too many US citizens are not aware of the wide disparities produced by unregulated capitalism (neoliberalism / corporate globalism). For example, in 2012 the world's one hundred wealthiest individuals added $241 billion to their bank accounts. They currently have a worth of $1.9 trillion: just a little less than the whole output of England. The fact that this happened is not an accident. The increase in the prosperity of the super wealthy is the direct result of legislation. Some of them include the decreasing of tax rates and tax enforcement, states' refusal to recover a fair share of revenues from minerals and land, privatization of public assets and the molding of a toll-booth economy, wage liberalization, and the dismantling of collective bargaining (Monbiot 2013). Our winner-take-all method is flailing away at previously healthy segments of society, leaving them like useless limbs on a convulsing body, even as the relative few that benefit support the delusion of opportunity and prosperity for everyone. Some rich and uninformed people label the lowest income, 47 percent of Americans, as the takers that benefit from state services at the expense of the high-earning 1 percent. These claims are hollow. The total amount paid out in welfare (TANF) is less than the investment income of three of the one percent of the wealthiest people in one year (Burcheit 2013; The Contributor 2014).

The monthly (Temporary Assistance for Needy Families) payment to a family of four is less than what the average member of the Forbes' top 20 made in one second on the job. The 47% do not own stocks—they don't own anything—and the so-called takers have zero wealth. The value of any assets owned by 47% of the nation is passed by their indebtedness. Uninformed people accuse recipients of entitlements of receiving something for nothing or being "on the fiddle." However, the opposite is the case. Statistics from the Urban Institute show that a two-earning family making average money through a life span will get less in social security than what they gave into the system. The same is also true for single men and almost equal for single women. Getting something for nothing? Deductions and exemptions that mainly help the highest-earning citizens cost approximately 8 percent of the gross domestic product, an identical amount that goes into social security and Medicare. If one of the tax breaks for the super rich, the $113,700 cap on payroll tax, were dismantled social security could be financed for the next seven decades (Burcheit 2013; The Contributor 2014).

REFERENCES

ABA (2013) "ABA Urges Steps to Curb Prison Overcrowding/Costs."

Abramovitz, Mimi. 2012. "Theorizing the Neoliberal Welfare State for Social Work."

Abramsky, Sasha. 2002. "Crime as America's Pop Culture." *The Chronicle of Higher Education* 21(2): B11–12.

ACLU. 2012. "Women in Prison." Retrieved from http// www.aclu.org/prisoners-rights/women-prison.

ACLU. 2011. "Banking on Bondage: Private Prisons and Mass Incarceration."

Alexander, Michelle. 2012. *The New Jim Crow: Mass Incarceration in the Age of Colorblindness.* New York: The New Press.

Michelle Alexander: Missile Strikes in Syria Will Be As Ill ... (n.d.). Retrieved from http://www.alternet.org/

civil-liberties/michelle-alexander-missile-strikes-syria-will-be-ill-fated-nations-punitive-justice

Allen, Francis. 1981. *The Decline of the Rehabilitative Ideal.* Yale University Press.

Allen, Howard W., and Jerome M. Clubb. 2008. *Race, Class, and the Death Penalty: Capital Punishment in American History.* SUNY Press.

Anand, Prerna. 2012. "Winners and Losers: Corrections and Higher Education in California." *California Common Sense.* Retrieved from http://www.cacs.org/ca/article/44.

Andrus, Tracy. 2012. "Characteristics of Successful Ex-Felons: A Microanalysis."

Anne Casey Foundation. "A Road Map for Juvenile Justice Reform." Retrieved from www.aecf.org.

Axinn, June, and Mark Stern. 2004. *Social Welfare: A History of American Response to Need.* 6th ed. Boston: Allyn and Bacon.

Balko, Radley. 2013. *Rise of the Warrior Cop: The Militarization of America's Police Forces.*

Barak, G., P. Leighton, and J. Flavin. 2010. *Class, Race, Gender & Crime: Social Realities of Justice in America.* Lanham, MD: Rowman & Littlefield.

Bernard, T., and S. Kurlychek. 2010. *The Cycle of Juvenile Justice*. Cary, NC: Oxford University Press.

Biron, Carey. 2013. "US Prison Population Seeing Unprecedented Increase." *Inter Press Service News Agency*. Retrieved from http://www.ipsnews. net/2013/02/.

Blau, J., and P. Blau. 2006. "Economic Inequality." *Journal of Criminal Justice* 34(5): 303–313.

Brent, J., and P. Kraska. 2010. *Theorizing Criminal Justice: Eight Essential Orientations*. Long Grove, Illinois: Waveland Press.

Bresler, R. J. (2008). "Liberalism's Third Act?" *USA Today (Society for the Advancement of Education)*. Retrieved July 28, 2010 from http:// findarticles.com/p/articles/mim1272/is2752316/ ain24258648/?tag=content;col1.

Bulloch, Heather, Karen F. Wyche, and Wendy R. Williams. 2001. "Media Images of the Poor." *Journal of Social Issues*, Vol. 57, No. 2: 229–246.

Bureau of Labor Statistics. 2002. "Local Area Unemployment Statistics" (Online Public Data Query). Retrieved March 1, 2003. http:// www,blr,gov/lan/home.htm.

Bushway, S. D., and S.G. Sweeten. 2007. "Abolish Lifetime Band for Ex-Felons." *Criminology and Public Policy* 6: 697–706.

Butler, Kate. 2006. "Portraying Poverty in the News."

Butterfield, Bob. "Government Spends More on Corporate Welfare Subsidies than Social Welfare Programs."

Bynum, T. S., B. A. Koons, and M. Morash. 1998. "Women Offenders: Programming Needs and Promising Approaches." *National Institute of Justice.* Washington DC.

Campbell, A., R. Berk, and J. Fyfe. 1998. "Deployment of Violence: The Los Angeles Police Department's Use of Dogs." *Evaluation Review*, 22: 535–6.

Campbell, John L. 2010. "Neoliberalism's Penal and Debtor States." *A Rejoinder to Loïc Wacquant.*

Chaddha, Anmol, and William Julius Wilson. 2011. "Way Down in the Hole: Systemic Urban Inequality and the Wire." *Critical Inquiry* 38(1): 1–23.

Cleland, John. 2010."Investigation of the Juvenile Justice Scandal in Luzerne County, Pennsylvania"

Clear, Todd. 2009. "The Collateral Consequences of Mass Incarceration." *Crime & Justice: A Review of Research* 37.

Covington S. Stephanie. 1998. "Women in Prison: Approaches in the Treatment of Our Most Invisible Populations.

Coyle, M. J. 2009. "Race and Class Penalties in Crack Cocaine Sentencing." Paper presented at annual meeting of the Sociological Association, Atlanta Hilton Hotel.

Curry, Elliot. 1998. *Crime and Punishment in America: Why the Solutions to America's Most Stubborn Social Crisis Have Not Worked and What Will.* New York: Metropolitan Books.

Dagenham and Leicester. 2006. *Poor Whites: The Forgotten Underclass.*

Dallas Indicator. 2013. "Crime & Safety: Fairness and Equity in the Criminal Justice System."

Danaher, D., and R. Schutt. 1982. "Race and Juvenile Justice Processing in Court and Police Agencies." *American Journal of Sociology*, 87: 1113–32.

Davis, Angela. 2008. "Locked Up: Racism in the Era of Neoliberalism." Retrieved from http://www.abc.

net.au/news/2008-03-19/locked-up-racism-in-the-era-of-neoliberalism/1077518.

Dowler, Kenneth. 2003. "Media Consumption and Public Attitudes Toward Crime and Justice: The Relationship Between Fear of Crime, Punitive Attitudes, and Perceived Police Effectiveness." *Journal of Criminal Justice and Popular Culture*, 10(2): 109–126.

Downs, Ray. 2013. "Who's Getting Rich off the Prison-Industrial Complex?"

Duncan, Cynthia M. 1992. *Rural Poverty in America*. New York: Greenwood Publishing Group.

Dunnaville, Clarence M. 2012. "Unequal Justice Under the Law—Racial Inequities in the Justice System." *Virginia Lawyer* 4(5): 20–25.

Ehrman, John. 2011. "Neoconservatism." Retrieved from http://www.firstprinciplesjournal.com/articles.

Equal Justice Initiative. 2010. United States Considered Most Punitive Country in the World.

Eslinger, Don, Torrey E. Fuller, Aaron D. Kennard, Richard Lamb, and James Pavle. 2010. "More Mentally Ill Persons Are in Jails and Prisons than Hospitals: A Survey of the States."

FAMM. 2013. "Sentences That Fit Justice That Works: Recent State Level Reforms to Mandatory Minimum Laws."

Forman, James. 2011. "Racial Critiques of Mass Incarceration: Beyond the New Jim Crow." *NYU Law Review.* Working Paper 243.

Focault, Michael. 1979. "The Birth of Biopolitics: Lectures at the College de France." *International Journal of Cultural Policy* 16: 56–57.

Fox, Richard L., Robert W. Van Sickel, and Thomas L. Steiger. 2007. *Tabloid Justice: Criminal Justice in an Age of Media Frenzy.* 2nd ed.

Freeman, Gregory. 1997. "Media Puts Black Face on Poverty (Media Portrayal of Poor Blacks)." *St. Louis Journalism Review.*

García, Arnoldo and Martinez, Elizabeth. 2000. "What is "Neo-Liberalism?A Brief Definition"

Gajwan, Seema. 2012. "Retire the Leeches: The Promise of Evidence-Based Solutions." *The Sentencing Project* 25(1): 44–45.

Garland, David. 2001. *The Culture of Control.* University of Chicago Press.

Geller, W. 1982 "Deadly force: What we know." *Journal of Police Science and Administration*, 10: 151–77.

Geller, Amanda, Irwin Garfinkel, and Bruce Western. 2011. "Incarceration and Support for Children in Fragile Families."

Geller, A., I. Garfinkel, and B. Western. 2011. "Invisible Men: Mass Incarceration and the Myth of Black Progress." *Demography* 48(1): 25–47.

George, Susan. 2013. "A Brief History of Neoliberalism." Znet. http://www.zmag.org/Spanish/0501geor.htm.

Gilens, Martin. 1999. "A Conversation about Welfare and the Media," May 17–31, Volume 27, Number 32.

Gillum, Jack. 2012. "Welfare Spending Nearly Half What US Forked Out in Corporate Subsidies in 2006." Study.

Giuseppe, Campesi. 2009. "Neoliberal and Neoconservative Discourses on Crime and Punishment." *Oñati Journal of Emergent Socio-Legal Studies*, Volume 3 Issue 1: 33–52.

Glaze, Lauren. 2009. "Correctional Populations in the United States, December 21, 2010." United States Bureau of Justice Statistics.

Gopnik, Adam. 2012. "The Caging of America: Why Do We Lock Up So Many People?"

Greenhouse, Linda. 1999. "47% in Poll View Legal System as Unfair to Poor and Minorities." Retrieved from http://www.nytimes.com/1999/02/24/us/47-in-poll-view-legal-system-as-unfair-to-poor-and-minorities.html.

Herzing, Rachel. 2005. "What Is the Prison-Industrial Complex?" *Critical Resistance.*

Steven Hawkins. 2010. "Education vs. Incarceration." *The American Prospect.*

Hepburn, J. 1978. "Race and the decision to arrest: An analysis of warrants issued." *Journal of Research in Crime and Delinquency*, 15: 54–73.

Hindelang, M. 1978. "Race and involvement in common-law personal crimes." *American Sociological Review*, 43: 93–109.

Holzer, Harry. 2003. "Employment Dimensions of Reentry: Understanding the Nexus between Prisoner Reentry and Work, Employment Barriers Facing Ex-Offenders."

Jackson, P. 1989. *Minority Group Threat, Crime, and Policing: Social Context and Social Control.* New York: Praeger.

Jacobs, D., and R. O'Brien. 1998. "The Determinants of Deadly Force: A Structural Analysis of Police Violence." *American Journal of Sociology*, 103: 837–62.

Johnson-Parris, Afi S. 2003. "Felon Disenfranchisement: The Unconscionable Social Contract Breached." *Virginia Law Review*, Vol. 89, No. 1: 109–138.

Karmen, A. 1990. *Crime Victims: An Introduction to Victimology.* Pacific Grove, CA: Brook/Cole Publishing Co.

Kleck, Gary. 1981. "Racial Discrimination in Criminal Sentencing: A Critical Evaluation of the Evidence with Additional Evidence on the Death Penalty." *American Sociological Review* Vol. 46, No. 6: 783–805.

"Labeling Theories of Crime." 2006. Retrieved from http://www.drtomoconnor.com/1060/1060lect07.htm.

Loo, Dennis. 2013. "Courting Catastrophe: Neoliberalism's Threat."

Kraska, Pete, and Victor E. Kappeler. 1997. "Militarizing American Police: The Rise and Normalization of Paramilitary Units."

LAO. 2005. "A Primer: Three Strikes—The Impact After More Than a Decade."

Leach, Molly. 2013. "Restorative Justice Is on the Rise."

Lee, Trymaine. 2012. "Recidivism Hard To Shake For Ex-Offenders Returning Home To Dim Prospects." Retrieved from http://www.huffingtonpost.com/2012/06/09/recidivism-harlem-convicts_n_1578935.html.

Liska, A., and M. Chamlin. 1984. "Social structure and crime control among macro social units." *American Journal of Sociology*, 90: 383–95.

Lopez, Ian H. 2003. "Racism on Trial: The Chicano Fight for Justice."

Manning, Marable. 2008. "Incarceration vs. Education: Reproducing Racism and Poverty in America."

Mauer, M. and M. Chesney-Lind. 2002. *Invisible Punishment: The Collateral Consequences of Mass Imprisonment.* New York: The New Press.

McCann, Bryan. 2007. *Fighting the Prison-Industrial Complex: A Call to Communication and Cultural Studies Scholars to Change the World.* University of Illinois Press.

McDonough, T., M. Reich, and D. Kotz. 2010. "Introduction: Social Structure of Accumulation Theory." In Contemporary Capitalism and Its Crises, edited by T. McDonough, M. Reich, and D. Kotz. New York: Cambridge University Press. 1–22.

Mead, Walter R. 2004. "The Decline of Fordism and the Challenge to American Power." Retrieved from http://www.digitalnpq.org/archive/2004_summer/mead.html

Merton, Robert. 1964. *Social Theory and Social Structure*. University of Minnesota: Free Press.

Miller, David W. 2010. "The Drain of Public Prison Systems and the Role of Privatization."

Monbiot, George. 2013. "If You Think We Are Done with Neoliberalism, Think Again."

The Guardian.

Monohan, Torin. 2006. "Surveillance and Security Technological Politics and Power in Everyday Life."

Moores, John. 2012. "Where is Penal Activism? Contesting the Neoliberal Prison Reclaim Justice Network." Retrieved from http:// downsizingcriminaljustice.

Moyers, Bill. 2007. "A Brief History of America's Penal Philosophy." PBS.

NAACP. 2011. Misplaced Priorities: Over Incarcerate, Under Educate Excessive. Spending on Incarceration Undermines Educational Opportunity and Public Safety in Communities

Navarro, Z. 2006. "In Search of Cultural Interpretation of Power." *IDS Bulletin* 37(6): 11–22.

Noisette, Leonard. 2012. "Resetting our Moral Compass: Devastated Communities Leading the Fight for a Just System." *The Sentencing Project* 25(1): 22–23.

O'Malley, Pat. 2008. *Neoliberalism and Risk in Criminology: The Critical Criminology Companion.* Sydney, Australia: Federation Press.

Palmer, Louise D. 1999. *The Boston Globe.* This article includes information from the *Seattle Post-Intelligencer* staff. This article appeared in the *Seattle Post-Intelligencer* Tuesday, March 2, Pages A-1 and A-4.

Parenti, Michael. 1992. *Make-Believe Media: The Politics of Entertainment.* New York: St. Martin's Press.

Parke, Ross, and K. Alison Clarke-Stewart. 2002. "Effects of Parental Incarceration on Young Children." Papers prepared for the "From Prison to Home" Conference, January 30–31, 2002.

Patchin, Justin W. 2004. "Alternatives to Incarceration: An Evidence-Based Research Review A Summary of Findings."

PBS Frontline Interview with John Langbein. 2004. Retrieved from http://www.pbs.org/wgbh/pages/frontline/shows/plea/interviews/langbein.html.

Pelaez, Vicky. 2013. "The Prison Industry in the United States: Big Business or a New Form of Slavery?"

Pettit, Becky. 2010. "Black Progress? Not When You Include the Incarcerated."

Philomena, Mariani. 2001. "Overview: Law, Order, and Neoliberalism." *Social Justice* 28:3 Popehat. 2013. "The Eric Holder Memorandum on Mandatory Minimum Sentences, Explained."

Political Gates. 2012. "Scandal in Lockdown Mode."

Pritchard, David. 1985. "Race, Homicide, and Newspapers." *Journalism Quarterly* 62 (4): 500–507.

Recoquillon, C., and **K. Sydenham**, K. 2006. "Democracy's Punishment: Felon Disenfranchisement." **http://xroads.virginia.edu/~class/trash/trash3.html.**

Reiman, J., and P. Leighton. 2010. *The Rich Get Rich and the Poor Get Prison: Ideology, Class, and Criminal Justice.* New York: Allyn & Bacon.

Robinson III, W. T. 2011. "Criminal Justice Reforms Enhance Public Safety and Strengthens Our Courts." *Trends in State Courts.* Retrieved from http://www.ncsc.org.

Rosich, Katherine. 2007. "Race, Ethnicity, and the Criminal Justice System." *American Sociological Association* 1: 1–23.

Rubin, Rachel. 2013. "Of Bankers, Pundits, and Hillbillies: Working Class Perspectives Commentary on Working Class Culture." *Education and Politics.* Retrieved from http://workingclassstudies.wordpress.com/.

Schiraldi, Vincent, and Geri Silva. 2004. "Old Three Strikes Law, Still Striking Out."

Sentencing Project. 2012. "Felon Voting Laws Disenfranchise 5.85 Million Americans With Criminal Records."

Sharp, Gwen. 2008. "Black/White Disparities in Prison Sentences."

Shaw, Greg M. 2007. "The Welfare Debate (Historical Guides to Controversial Issues in America)."

Sherman, Lawrence W. 2001. "Trust and Confidence in Criminal Justice."

Siddiqui, Sabrina. 2013. Ron Paul: Shutdown After Boston Bombings More Frightening Than Attack Itself. The Huffington Post

Simmons, Charlene W. 2000. "Children of Incarcerated Parents."

Simon, Jonathan. 2010. *Clearing the "Troubled Assets" of America's Punishment Bubble.* The American Academy of Arts & Sciences.

Smith, D. 1986. "The Neighborhood Context of Police Behavior." In *Communities and Crime*, edited by A. Reiss Jr. and M. Tonry. Chicago: University of Chicago Press.

Spohn, Cassia. 2000. Thirty Years of Sentencing Reform: The Quest for a Racially Neutral Sentencing Process. *Criminal Justice, National Institute of Justice* Vol. 3: 427–501; 453

Stevenson, Bryan. 2013. "Drug Policy, Criminal Justice, and Mass Imprisonment." Working paper prepared for the first meeting of the commission, Geneva.

Stier, Ken. 2009. "Getting the Juvenile-Justice System to Grow Up."

Taylor, Marisa. 2010. "Racial Disparities in Sentencing Rise after Guidelines Loosened." *McClatchy Newspapers.*

Texas Department of Public Safety. 2000. Executive Summary: TRAFFICSTOPDATAREPORT.

Tierney, John. 2013. "Time and Punishment: Prison Population Can Shrink When Police Crowd Streets." *New York Times.*

Tucker, Susan B. 2012. "The Elephant in the Room: The Necessity of Race and Class Consciousness." *The Sentencing Project* 25(1): 7–8.

Uggen, Christopher, and Sarah Shannon. 2012. "State Level Estimates of Felon Disenfranchisement in the United States, 2010."

Vogel, Richard D. 2009. "Dismantling the Prison House of Nations: A Socialist Prison Reform Proposal." *Monthly Review Foundation.* Retrieved from http://mrzine.monthlyreview.org/.

Vogel, Richard D. 2009. "Globalization and the Incarceration of the Black Working Class: An In-Depth Political Analysis."

Volunteers of America. 2013. "Look Up and Hope: Strengthening Families Affected by Incarceration."

Vosters, Helene. 1999. "Media Lockout: Prisons and Journalists." *Media Alliance*. Retrieved from http://www.media-alliance.org/article.php?id=539.

Wacquant, Loic. 1999. "Prisons of Poverty."

Wacquant, Loic. 2001. "From Slavery to Mass Incarceration: Rethinking the Race Question in the United States." *New Left Review* 13(7): 41–60.

Wacquant, Loic. 2000. "The New Peculiar Institution: The Prison as a Surrogate Ghetto." *Theoretical Criminology* 4 (3): 377–389.

Wacquant, L. 1998. "From Welfare State to Prison State: Imprisoning The American Poor."

Washington, Laura. 2008. "Missing Minorities in the Media." *In These Times* 37(4): 35–41.

Weinberg, Bruce. 2002. "Higher Crime Rate Linked to Low Wages and Unemployment, Study Finds."

Western, Bruce and Christopher Wildeman. 2011. "Incarceration in Fragile Families."

Western, Bruce. 2007. *Crime, Punishment, and American Inequality*. New York: The Russell Sage Foundation.

Western, Bruce. 2004. *Politics and Social Structure In the Culture of Control*. Florence, KY: Routledge-Taylor & Francis Group. 2004.

Western, Bruce. 2005. "Punishment and Inequality in America." *Socio-economics Review* 5(3): 569–586.

Western, B., and B. Pettit. 2010. "Incarceration and Social Inequality." *Labor Relations Review* 54(4): 3–16.

Welch, R., and C. Angulo. *Justice on Trial: Racial Disparities in the American Criminal Justice System.* Washington D.C.: Leadership Conference on Civil Rights. 2000.

Wheelock, D, and C. Uggen. 2006. "Race, Poverty, and Punishment: The Impact of Criminal Sanctions on Racial, Ethnic, and Socioeconomic Inequality." Retrieved from http://www.npc.umich.edu/publications/workingpaper06.

Wilbanks, William. 1987. *The Myth of a Racist Criminal Justice System*. Monterey, CA: Brooks/Cole Publishing Company.

Wilderman, C., and B. Western. 2010. "Incarceration in Fragile Families." *Future of Children* 20(2): 157–177.

Wilson, Christopher P. 2010 "Learning to Live with Crime: American Crime Narrative in the Neoconservative Turn."

Williams, Natasha H. 2013. "Silent Victims: The Impact of Parental Incarceration on Children."

Wilson, Amanda. 2011. "US: For Many Women, a Prison Sentence Also Means Abuse."

Wright, Paul. 2007. "The Crime of Being Poor." *Prison Legal News* 16.(5): 45–46.

Zafirovski, Milan. 2008. *Modern Free Society and Its Nemesis: Political and Economic Freedoms and their Antithesis in the Third Millenium.* Landham, MD: Lexington Books–Rowman & Litlefield.

Zheng, Jialing. "The Abuse-Incarceration Connection." Women out of Prison, A

Project of the News &Documentary graduate program at the Arthur L. Carter Journalism Institute of New York University